Learn Every Day About Shapes

Edited by Kathy Charner

Learn Every Day
About SHAPES

BEST IDEAS from TEACHERS

EDITED BY
Kathy Charner

© 2009 Gryphon House, Inc.
Published by Gryphon House, Inc.
PO Box 207, Beltsville, MD 20704
800.638.0928; 301.595.9500; 301.595.0051 (fax)

Visit us on the web at www.gryphonhouse.com

Illustrations: Deb Johnson
Cover Art: Stock photos

Library of Congress Cataloging-in-Publication Information:
Learn every day about shapes / edited by Kathy Charner.
    p. cm.
 ISBN 978-0-87659-092-8
1. Shapes--Study and teaching (Preschool)--Activity programs. 2.
Geometry--Study and teaching (Preschool)--Activity programs. 3.
Shapes--Study and teaching (Early childhood)--Activity programs. 4.
Geometry--Study and teaching (Early childhood)--Activity programs. I.
Charner, Kathy.
 QA461.L43 2009
 516'.15--dc22

                                    2009001246

BULK PURCHASE
Gryphon House books are available for special premiums and sales promotions as well as for fund-raising use. Special editions or book excerpts also can be created to specification. For details, contact the Director of Marketing at Gryphon House.

DISCLAIMER
Gryphon House, Inc. and the authors cannot be held responsible for damage, mishap, or injury incurred during the use of or because of activities in this book. Appropriate and reasonable caution and adult supervision of children involved in activities and corresponding to the age and capability of each child involved is recommended at all times. Do not leave children unattended at any time. Observe safety and caution at all times.

Table of Contents

Note: The books listed in the Related Children's Books section of each activity may occasionally include books that are only available used or through your local library.

Introduction

You have in your hands a great teacher resource! This book, which is part of the *Learn Every Day* series, contains 100 activities you can share with children ages 3–6 to help them develop a lifelong love of learning, as well as the knowledge and skills all children need to become successful students in kindergarten and beyond. The activities in this book are written by teachers and professionals from the field of early childhood education—educators and professionals who use these activities in their classrooms every day.

The activities in this book are separated by curriculum areas, such as Art, Dramatic Play, Outdoor Play, Small Motor, and so on, and are organized according to their age appropriateness, so activities best suited for children ages three and up come first, then activities for children age four and up, and finally, activities for children age five and up. Each activity has the following components—learning objectives, a list of related vocabulary words, a list of thematically related books, a list of the materials (if any) you need to complete the activity, directions for preparation, and the activity itself. Also included in each activity is an assessment component to help you observe how well the children are meeting the learning objectives. Given the emphasis on accountability in early childhood education, these assessment strategies are essential.

Several activities also contain teacher-to-teacher tips that provide smart and useful ideas, including how to expand the central idea of an activity in a new way or where to find the materials necessary to complete a given activity. Some activities also include related fingerplays, poems, or songs that you can sing and chant with the children. Children love singing, dancing, and chanting—actions that help expand children's understanding of an activity's learning objectives.

This book, and the other books in this series, give early childhood educators 100 great activities that require few materials, little if any preparation, and are sure to make learning fun and engaging for children.

Circle Painting

3+

LEARNING OBJECTIVES

The children will:
1. Identify circles.
2. Create paintings with circles.

Materials

white construction
    paper
tempera paint in a
    variety of colors
plastic cups in a
    variety of sizes
pie tins

VOCABULARY

circle   cup   paint   round

PREPARATION

● Pour the tempera paint into the pic tins, using one color per tin.

WHAT TO DO

1. Place the paint-filled pie tins and plastic cups in the middle of the table, and provide each child with a piece of white construction paper.
2. Ask the children to look at the top of each cup and help the children identify the shape they see.
3. Have the children dip the plastic cups in the tempera paint and then press them onto their paper. Encourage the children to use different colors to create many circle designs.
4. Let their paintings dry, and then hang them in a prominent place in the classroom.

FINGERPLAY

Make a Circle by Laura Wynkoop
Make a circle
In the sky. (use index finger to draw a circle in the air)
Stretch to make one
Way up high. (stand up on your toes and draw a circle over your head)
Move your arm, (make a circle with your arm)
And move your hand. (make a circle with your hand)
Make a circle
Big and grand. (make the biggest circle you can make)

Children's Books

Around the Park: A Book About Circles by Christianne C. Jones
Circles by Diyan Leake
Circles by Marybeth Lorbiecki

ASSESSMENT

To assess the children's learning, consider the following:
● Can each child identify the shapes she painted?
● Can each child spot other circles in the room?

Laura Wynkoop, San Dimas, CA

Circles in Circles

3+

LEARNING OBJECTIVES

The children will:
1. Learn to identify circles.
2. Use their large motor skills.

Materials

several 6-ounce
  and 15-counce
  cans with both
  ends removed
  and rough edges
  smoothed out
paint in basic
  colors
scissors (adult only)
shallow pans
various colored
  sheets of
  construction
  paper
can opener
tape
set of shape
  flashcards

VOCABULARY

circle	dip	print	round
different	paint		

PREPARATION

- Cut 12" circles out of various colored sheets of construction paper.
- Use the can opener on empty 6-ounce and 15-counce cans to remove both ends.
- Make sure the rough edges are smoothed out and taped over, if necessary, so no little hands will be cut.

WHAT TO DO

1. Pour the paint in small shallow pans.
2. Show the children how to dip the end of a can into the paint and print a circle on their circle papers. Encourage them to print several circles without dipping the can into the paint again.
3. Remind the children to use different sizes of cans, trying to fit the print of a smaller can into the print of a larger can. Also, remind them not to slide the can to keep the circle clear and easy to see.

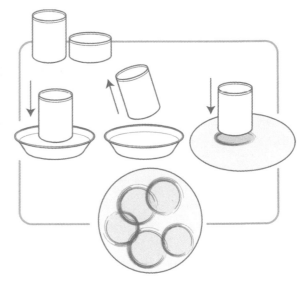

TEACHER-TO-TEACHER TIP

- Eat a snack of circle-shaped cereal on round plates or bowls.

ASSESSMENT

To assess the children's learning, consider the following:
- Show the children a group of shapes and ask them to find all the circles.
- Can the children use the cans to make circles without smudging them?

Susan Oldham Hill, Lakeland, FL

Children's Books

Circles, Triangles, and Squares by Tana Hoban
My Very First Book of Shapes by Eric Carle
When a Line Bends…A Shape Begins by Rhonda Gowler Greene

Edible Shape Art

3+

LEARNING OBJECTIVES

The children will:
1. Classify objects by shape.
2. Coordinate eye-hand movement by manipulating materials in a purposeful way.
3. Understand and follow verbal directions.

VOCABULARY

circle	imagination	semi-circle	square
create	rectangle	shapes	triangle
gallery	rhombus	spiral	

WHAT TO DO

1. Ask all the children to wash their hands before starting the art project. Supply all children with a big paper plate to work on. Also supply an edible adhesive (chocolate syrup works well), a craft stick, and edible shapes. Be sure to name all the shapes while introducing the project.
2. Invite the children to design creative shape art. If some children are having trouble coming up with ideas, provide suggestions to get them started. Possible shape art ideas include ice cream cones, cars, houses, animals, rainbows, people, flowers, and so on.
3. After the children finish their work and clean up, have "gallery time," and encourage every "artist" explain what she did.
4. With the children, count the number of shapes in each art project. For older children, consider expanding this activity by asking them to keep a tally of all the shapes they use.
5. When the children are finished counting the numbers of edible shapes they made, invite them to eat the their shapes. Encourage the children to count the edible shapes as they eat their creations

TEACHER-TO-TEACHER TIP

- Take pictures of all the projects. Hang them on a clothesline for display in your classroom.

ASSESSMENT

To assess the children's learning, consider the following:
- Record what the children say about the various designs and shapes.
- Observe individual small motor skills. Keep track of the children's progress by using informal notes.

Freya Zellerhoff, Towson, MD

Materials

big paper plate (one per child)
chocolate syrup for edible glue, use sparingly (fill in small containers rather than passing big bottles along)
craft sticks or plastic spoons to apply edible glue
edible shapes
edible glue, such as royal icing that is used to create gingerbread houses

Children's Books

Mouse Shapes by Ellen Stoll Walsh
The Shape of Things by Ann Dayle Dodds
Ship Shapes by Stella Blackstone
So Many Circles, So Many Shapes by Tana Hoban

Crayon Resist Shapes

4+

LEARNING OBJECTIVES

The children will:
1. Learn to identify a circle, triangle, square, and rectangle.
2. Learn to use stencils.

scissors (adult only)
tagboard shape
    stencils
thinned blue paint
paintbrushes
construction paper
yellow and orange
    crayons

VOCABULARY

circle   square   stencil   triangle
rectangle

PREPARATION

- To make stencils, cut 3" shapes (circles, triangles, squares, and rectangles) from the center of 5" square pieces of tagboard, leaving a wide border around the cutout area.
- Prepare a thin blue wash by adding water to blue paint. Practice painting it over paper marked with yellow crayon to make sure it is thin enough to bead up on the paint.

WHAT TO DO

1. Show the children how to color a shape inside the stencil. Encourage them to press down with the yellow and orange crayons to make bright shapes.

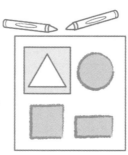
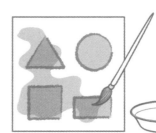

2. Repeat coloring the shapes until the children use every shape at least once on their papers.
3. Show them how to paint with the thinned wash across the papers from left to right. Encourage them to go all the way across without repainting an area to avoid having the paint cover the stenciled shapes.

ASSESSMENT

To assess the children's learning, consider the following:
- Show the children shape flashcards and ask them to name the shapes.
- Can the children identify the shapes they used the stencils to paint?

Susan Oldham Hill, Lakeland, FL

Children's Books

All Shapes and Sizes by John J. Reiss
Circles, Triangles, and Squares by Tana Hoban

Negative Space

Materials

paper
scissors (adult only)
paint
easel(s)

LEARNING OBJECTIVES

The children will:
1. Gain an understanding of negative space.
2. Develop their small motor skills.

VOCABULARY

imagination   line   negative space   shape

PREPARATION

● On large pieces of easel paper, cut one small hole in each paper. The shape can be any geometric shape or an abstract shape and can be anywhere on the page.

WHAT TO DO

1. Fasten a piece of paper to the easel and ask the children to use paint to create around the negative space. **Note:** This activity also works well on tabletops.
2. Without giving directions, let the children decide what they want to do with that space. There is no right or wrong. Rather, this is a chance for the children to create and think about their process.
3. Also consider adding cutout shapes to glue on the paper as an extension on another day. You can also put shapes cut out from dark-colored paper behind the white paper so that the shapes show through. What will the children do with that shape now?

TEACHER-TO-TEACHER TIP

● Children do not need to make a recognizable creation with the shape. The process is more important than making a recognizable product.

ASSESSMENT

To assess the children's learning, consider the following:
● Ask each child which shape he would like cut out of the paper before he paints. Hold up a shape and ask if it is the shape he named. Then see if he recognizes that shape by name.
● If shown a shape or told a shape name, can each child find similarly shaped objects in the room?

Laura Durbrow, Lake Oswego, OR

Children's Books

Bear in a Square by Stella Blackstone
Color Farm by Lois Ehlert
Mouse Shapes by Ellen Stoll Walsh
Twizzlers: Shapes and Patterns by Jerry Pallotta

One-Shape Pictures

4+

LEARNING OBJECTIVES

The children will:
1. Put ideas they have into practice.
2. Understand and follow directions and answer questions.

Materials

lots of construction
    paper in
    different colors
scissors (adult only)
white paper
glue sticks

VOCABULARY

circle	heptagon	pentagon	spiral
create	imagination	rectangle	square
gallery	octagon	semi-circle	triangle

WHAT TO DO

1. Engage the children in a discussion to decide on the single shape they will use in this art project. Use a basic shape like a triangle, square, rectangle, or circle.
2. Cut several shapes in different sizes from a variety of paper.
3. Encourage the children to think of creative ways they can make pictures using colorful shapes. For example, if the children are using circles, they could put them together to make a colorful flower garden, a snowman family, and so on. Also, consider doing "modern" shape art: experiment with putting several different-sized shapes next to each other or on top of each other.
4. Have "gallery time," and give each child a chance to talk about his artwork.

ASSESSMENT

To assess the children's learning, consider the following:
- Include shape artwork in portfolio documentation. Include the children's input (for example, record what the children say about their artwork at gallery time).
- Ask the children questions about shapes at the beginning and again the end of the activity. Use visual clues if necessary (for example, if children are having trouble identifying a rectangle, say, "A rectangle looks like a door").

Freya Zellerhoff, Towson, MD

Children's Books

Shape Capers by
Cathryn Falwell
The Shape of Things by
Dayle Ann Dodds
When a Line Bends...A Shape Begins
by Rhonda
Gowler Greene

Symmetrical Shapes

LEARNING OBJECTIVES

The children will:

1. Learn to identify a square, rectangle, triangle, circle, and oval.
2. Learn about symmetry.

Materials

scissors (adult only)
construction paper
red, yellow, and
   blue paint
brushes
newspapers

VOCABULARY

shape names   symmetry

PREPARATION

● Cut construction paper into various 9" x 12" shapes.
● Set out newspaper over the area where the children will be working.

WHAT TO DO

1. Engage the children in a discussion about symmetry. Show the children how to fold a paper circle in half, and how it remains symmetrical. Then fold a triangle in half in a way that it asymmetrical.
2. Give the children paper shapes to fold in half, and then reopen and lay flat.
3. Provide paint and brushes. Invite the children to put dabs of paint on one side of the folds on their papers. Remind the children not to brush the paint around, but merely to dab them.
4. After they have put a few dabs of different colors of paint on their papers, direct the children to refold the paper, pressing hard several times on the paper. Help the children carefully reopen the paper so they can see the symmetrical dabs of paint on both sides of the paper.

TEACHER-TO-TEACHER TIP

● Consider taking the children on a walk through the school or the neighborhood to look for examples of symmetrical objects. Take notes or photographs of the symmetrical objects for the children to discuss later in the classroom.

ASSESSMENT

To assess the children's learning, consider the following:

● Does the child understand symmetry and asymmetry when you show him the difference with paper shapes?
● Can the child fold, paint, and press the paper to create symmetrical images?

Susan Oldham Hill, Lakeland, FL

Children's Books

All Shapes and Sizes by
John J. Reiss
*Circles, Triangles, and
Squares* by Tana Hoban
Color Dance by
Ann Jonas
*Is It Red? Is It Yellow? Is
It Blue?* by Tana Hoban
The Art Lesson by
Tomie dePaola

Block Tracings

5+

LEARNING OBJECTIVES

The children will:

1. Discover that shapes exist in many places.
2. Identify shapes that compose real objects.
3. Discuss the properties of various shapes.

Materials

small geometric
    blocks (or other
    small traceable
    shapes)
pencils
white paper
crayons or markers

VOCABULARY

angles   points   square   triangle
curves

WHAT TO DO

1. Explain to the children that basic shapes form most things in our world. Demonstrate by drawing a house made from a triangle and a square. Point out these shapes to the children using terms like "angles," "points," and "curves."
2. Ask the children to help you look around the room for basic shapes.
3. Provide each child with a handful of various blocks.
4. Ask the children to place the blocks on the paper, making specific shapes, and then trace around the blocks.
5. They can add extra details and color with the crayons.
6. Encourage the children to share and discuss what they are doing with each other. Ask questions such as, "What makes a triangle a good shape for a roof?" or "I wonder why you used a circle for a face."

TEACHER-TO-TEACHER TIP

● Tracing will leave pencil marks on the blocks. Either use old blocks or ones made with easily cleaned surfaces.

ASSESSMENT

To assess the children's learning, consider the following:

● Can the children name the shapes they are using?
● Can the children pair shapes in many combinations?
● Can the children state properties of shapes (for example, "circles are smooth and round")?

Jaclyn Miller, Mishawaka, IN

Children's Books

Block City by
Robert Louis Stevenson
Houses and Homes by
Ann Morris
*So Many Circles, So
Many Squares* by
Tana Hoban

Name Placemat

5+

LEARNING OBJECTIVES

The children will:

1. Learn to draw circles.
2. Begin to recognize the alphabet letters in their names.

Materials

plastic curtain rings
laminator
crayons
tag board
scissors (adult only)

VOCABULARY

circle   outline   placemat   square

PREPARATION

● Cut the tag board into pieces about the size of placemats.

WHAT TO DO

1. Give every child a piece of tag board, a curtain ring, and a few crayons.
2. Demonstrate how to use a curtain ring and crayon to draw a pattern with circles (for example, five circles in a row).
3. Help the children draw the outline of the circles (one for every letter in their name) on both the sides of the placemat and color them. Help the children write their names inside the circles (one circle for every letter).
4. Laminate the children's placemats for durability and send them home.

ASSESSMENT

To assess the children's learning, consider the following:

● Ask the children to point out circular objects in the classroom.
● Ask the children to use their index fingers to draw circles in the sand and water table or in the sandbox.

Shyamala Shanmugasundaram, Mumbai, India

Children's Books

Cheerios Counting Book by Barbara Barbieri McGrath
Shapes by Philip Yenawine
So Many Circles, So Many Squares by Tana Hoban

Shape Animals

5+

LEARNING OBJECTIVES

The children will:

1. Create an animal using geometric shapes cut from paper.
2. Use and be able to name at least three different shapes.
3. Use and be able to name at least two different colors.
4. Practice small motor skills by using scissors, crayons, and glue.

Materials

construction paper in a variety of colors
white construction paper
child-safe scissors
glue
crayons

VOCABULARY

circle	identify	rectangle	square
create	imagination	shapes	triangle

PREPARATION

- Draw a variety of shapes on the pieces of construction paper.
- Cut out some of the shapes for the younger children.

WHAT TO DO

1. Show the children a piece of construction paper with the shapes drawn on it. Point to the shapes and ask the children to identify them.
2. Help the children cut the shapes out and glue them on a piece of white paper to make an animal.
3. Encourage the children to use at least three different shapes to make their animals and at least two different colors of shapes. To check for understanding as the children work, ask them to name the different shapes and colors they are using.
4. Provide crayons so the children can add details to their animals, such as eyes, ears, stripes, and spots.
5. When each child finishes making an animal, ask her to identify the animal she has made. Write the name of the animal at the top of the child's paper.

TEACHER-TO-TEACHER TIP

- This lesson is primarily a large group activity, but can work very well with a small group. Also consider making a center of the activity by adding a set of picture directions that the children can follow in addition to instructions.

ASSESSMENT

To assess the children's learning, consider the following:

- Can each child use the shapes to create an animal?
- Can each child use and name at least three different shapes and two different colors?
- Are each child's small motor skills age appropriate?

Children's Books

Circles, Triangles, and Squares by Tana Hoban
Color Zoo by Lois Ehlert
Oodles of Animals by Lois Ehlert

Angela Rathbun, Centennial, CO

Three Dimensions

LEARNING OBJECTIVES

The children will:
1. Gain awareness of depth and flatness
2. Learn more about shapes.

Materials

shapes (circles, triangles, and squares) cut from construction paper
squares and cubes (wood blocks or plastic manipulative cubes)
circles and spheres (balls)
triangles and pyramids
ovals and egg-shaped objects

VOCABULARY

| cube | pyramid | sphere | three-dimensional |
| flat | round | | |

WHAT TO DO

1. Show the children a construction paper square and engage them in a conversation about the shape. Challenge the children to identify the shape's name. Explain to the children that construction paper squares are flat. Pass around the flat object.
2. Now, introduce a cube. Look at the six sides, count them aloud with the children and ask if they know the shape. Pass the cube around and have the children feel the sides of the object. Ask, "Is the cube flat too?" Teach the children that it is three-dimensional.
3. Do the same type of comparison with circles and spheres (use a picture of an orange and a real orange), and continue with the other flat and three-dimensional shapes.
4. Reinforce the concept by putting all the flat shapes together in a pile and having the children match the shape to the three-dimensional object.

ASSESSMENT

To assess the children's learning, consider the following:
● When the children examine flat and three-dimensional objects, do they know the difference, and can they describe how the two objects are different?

Patrick Mitchell, Yagoto, Nagoya, Japan

Children's Books

Flat Stanley by Jeff Brown
What's Inside? Toys by Angela Royston

Windows—Many Shapes and Sizes 5+

Materials

art paper
crayons
pencils
pictures of
   windows, cut
   from magazines

LEARNING OBJECTIVES

The children will:
1. Learn about different shapes and sizes of windows.
2. Identify the shapes of windows at school and at home.
3. Learn the names of various shapes, including "rectangular."

VOCABULARY

big	round	small	tall
rectangle	short	square	

PREPARATION

● Set art paper, crayons, and pencils on the tables.
● Set out the pictures of windows cut out from magazines.

WHAT TO DO

1. Show the children the pictures of windows. Talk with the children about various shapes of windows. Ask the children to identify some of the shapes.
2. Ask the children to draw pictures of windows. Encourage the children to draw images of the windows in the classroom, the windows from their homes, or to make drawings based on the images laid out before them. Some children might want to make several drawings. Some might want to draw and color frames or curtains, or even flowers on the windowsills.
3. Help the children write their names on their drawings. Challenge those children who are able to try writing their names themselves.
4. When the children finish working, engage them in a conversation about their drawings.
5. Display the papers on the wall for all to see. Keep the drawings up until the end of the week. Encourage the children to show the pictures they drew to their family.

ASSESSMENT

To assess the children's learning, consider the following:
● Can the children identify the shapes of the classroom windows?
● Can the children describe the windows at their homes?
● Show the children pictures of various kinds of windows. Can they identify the shapes?

Children's Books

My Very First Book of Shapes by Eric Carle
Outside My Window: A Children's Poetry Book by Fannie's Girl
The Shape of Things by Dandi Daley Mackall

Shirley Anne Ramaley, Sun City, AZ

Shape Detective

4+

LEARNING OBJECTIVES

The children will:
1. Identify shapes.
2. Improve their oral language skills.
3. Develop an appreciation for literature.

Materials

magnifying glass
baseball cap or
    other hat
children's
    magazines

VOCABULARY

book	hat	magazine
detective	identify	magnifying glass

PREPARATION

● Create a "detective cap" by attaching a few colorful paper or foam shapes to it.
● Display this "detective cap," magazines, and a magnifying glass at a table.

WHAT TO DO

1. Invite each child to have a turn to be a shape detective.
2. Have the children take turns donning the hat, selecting a magazine, and picking up the magnifying glass.
3. Each child searches through the magazine and identifies various shapes as she looks through the magnifying glass.
4. Talk with the children about the shapes they see in the magazine. Can the children recall other objects that have similar shapes?

SONG

I'm a Shape Detective by Mary J. Murray
(Tune "I'm a Little Teapot")

I'm a shape detective, (point to self)
Yes I am. (nod head, hands on hips)
I look for shapes (hand above eyes as if looking far off into distance)
Whenever I can.

I can find a shape
That's here (right hand out palm up)
Or there. (left hand out palm up)
I find shapes everywhere. (hand above eyes as if looking far off into distance)

Children's Books

Circles by
Janie Spaht Gill
Exploring Shapes by
Andrew King
See a Square by
Ben Mahan

ASSESSMENT

To assess the children's learning, consider the following:
● Invite one child to sit with you as she uses the "detective hat" and magnifying glass to identify various shapes on the pages of the magazine. Ask the child questions as she looks for shapes.
● Challenge the children look through paper towel tubes to locate and identify shapes in the classroom.

Mary J. Murray, Mazomanie, WI

Shape Glasses

4+

LEARNING OBJECTIVES

The children will:
1. Recognize shapes.
2. Develop their language skills.

Materials

two or more pairs
 of plastic
 sunglasses or toy
 eyeglasses
glue gun (adult
 only)
small colorful foam
 shapes
books

VOCABULARY

book	eyeglasses	look	see
eyes	glasses	read	shapes

PREPARATION

- Create several pair of shape glasses. Use the glue gun to attach a variety of foam shapes around the lenses of the sunglasses. Let dry.
- Display the pairs of shape glasses in the book corner, along with an assortment of books about shapes.

WHAT TO DO

1. Invite two or more children to put on a pair of the shape glasses.
2. Encourage the children to look through the glasses as they "read" the books about shapes.
3. Invite children to talk about the shapes they see on the pages of the books.

SONG

Shape Glasses Song by Mary J. Murray
(Tune: "Skip to My Lou")

Put on the glasses, look around. (child
 walks around the circle wearing
 glasses)
Put on the glasses, look around.
Put on the glasses, look around,
Tell us what you see.

I see a _____ looking at me. (child
 points to shape in room and says its
 name)
I see a _____ looking at me.
I see a _____ looking at me.
That is what I see.

Children's Books

Libby's New Glasses by
 Tricia Tusa
*Luna and the Big Blur: A
 Story for Children Who
 Wear Glasses* by
 Shirley Day
To See or Not to See by
 Steve Struble

ASSESSMENT

To assess the children's learning, consider the following:
- Look through a book with a child and invite her to point out and identify various shapes on the pages of the book.
- Invite one child to wear the shape glasses and walk around the room pointing to various shapes. The rest of the children watch and identify the shapes as the child selects them.

Mary J. Murray, Mazomanie, WI

Name That Shape

LEARNING OBJECTIVES

The children will:

1. Learn how to distinguish between shapes.
2. Learn how to spot shapes in everyday objects.

Materials

box
everyday objects, in a variety of shapes

VOCABULARY

circle	shapes	square	triangle

rectangle

WHAT TO DO

1. Call the children to circle or group time, and show them your box of objects.
2. Explain that there are shapes all around us, and point out a few in the classroom.
3. Then, tell the children that you have more shapes in your box.
4. Pull the first object out of the box, and ask the children if they can identify its shape.
5. Continue in this manner until the children identify all of the shapes in the box.

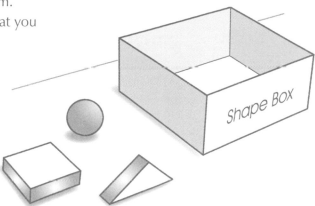

ASSESSMENT

To assess the children's learning, consider the following:

● Ask the children to recall and describe the shapes of the objects that they saw.
● Send the children on a mission to find other shapes in the classroom. Review and discuss the shapes that they find.

Erin Huffstetler, Maryville, TN

Children's Books

A Circle Here, a Square There by David Diehl
The Shape of Me and Other Stuff by Dr. Seuss
The Shape of Things by Dayle Ann Dodds

Erase a Shape

4+

LEARNING OBJECTIVES

The children will:

1. Learn to recognize a circle, triangle, square, and rectangle.
2. Develop their small motor skills.

Materials

chalk or dry-erase markers
chalkboard or dry-erase board
shape cards for circles, triangles, squares, and rectangles in a small bag or envelope

VOCABULARY

circle   rectangle   square   triangle

PREPARATION

● Make shape cards for circles, triangles, squares, and rectangles.
● Draw large shapes on the dry-erase board or chalkboard.

WHAT TO DO

1. Gather the children together and engage them in a discussion about the differences between shapes.
2. Choose a child to go to the chalkboard or dry-erase board where the shapes are drawn.
3. Call out a shape for the child to find and erase.
4. Repeat with a different child and different shape.

TEACHER-TO-TEACHER TIP

● Extend this activity by adding more shapes: oval, star, heart, diamond.

ASSESSMENT

To assess the children's learning, consider the following:

● Can each child correctly identify the names of the shapes?
● Can the child erase all of the correct shape without erasing the shapes nearby?

Susan Oldham Hill, Lakeland, FL

Children's Books

All Shapes and Sizes by John J. Reiss
The Art Lesson by Tomie dePaola
Listen to the Shape by Marcia Brown
Shapes by Guy Smalley

Secret Shapes

4+

LEARNING OBJECTIVES

The children will:

1. Learn about shapes.
2. Learn patterns through shapes.
3. Learn how to make shapes.

Materials

stencils of shapes
like squares,
circles, triangles
and rectangles
posters of shapes
on the wall
child-safe scissors
markers

VOCABULARY

| circle | pattern | square | trace |
| rectangle | shape | stencils | triangle |

PREPARATION

● Provide child-safe scissors and shape stencils and markers for each child.

WHAT TO DO

1. Cut shapes from paper for demonstration purposes. Draw another shape on the back of one the cut-out shapes.
2. Say, "We are going to draw a different shape on the back of this shape. It is a secret shape for now."
3. Ask the children to cut their shapes from the paper.
4. Help the children write their names and the names of their secret shapes on the backs of the cut-out shapes.
5. During circle or group time, ask the children to put their shapes up in the air, and then to turn their shapes around to reveal their secret shapes.
6. Ask each child to say the name of his secret shape aloud.
7. Collect all the shapes and place them in a pile. Create patterns from the shapes within the circle.

FINGERPLAY

Shape Play by Lily Erlic

Hold up a shape, (place shape in hand)
Hold it in the air! (stretch arm up with shape)
Wave it around, (wave the shape)
And give it a stare. (look at your shape)

Hold up a shape, (place shape in hand)
Stretch it up high, (stretch arm up with shape)
Give it a shake, (shake shape)
And watch it fly! (toss shape up in the air)

Children's Books

A Circle Here, a Square There by David Diehl
Shapes, Shapes, Shapes by Tana Hoban
Shapes & Patterns by Play Bac Edu-Team

ASSESSMENT

To assess the children's learning, consider the following:

● Can the children say the names of the shapes?
● Can the children place the shapes in the correct place?

Lily Erlic, Victoria, British Columbia, Canada

The Shapes Planet

4+

LEARNING OBJECTIVES

The children will:
1. Identify geometric shapes.
2. Make choices about materials.
3. Create three-dimensional arrangements.

Materials

scissors (adult only)
yarn
flannel board
felt squares,
   triangles, and
   circles of various
   sizes
googly eyes (at
   least three pairs)
Velcro

VOCABULARY

| alien | imagine | shape | triangle |
| circle | planet | square | |

PREPARATION

● Cut the yarn into matching lengths of 4", 6", and 8".
● Attach Velcro to the backs of googly eyes.

WHAT TO DO

1. Put the felt circles on the flannel board. Ask the children to identify the shape. Repeat this step with triangles and squares.
2. Put a large circle on the board and say, "This is the body of an alien from the shapes planet." Show children the yarn, eyes, and other shapes. Say, "Can you help me make the rest of the alien?"
3. Have children take turns adding felt pieces, eyes, and yarn to the circle to make an alien. Repeat with other shapes, encouraging the children to name the shapes, and to imagine the planets from which they come.

SONG

Look What We Can Make with Shapes by Cassandra Reigel Whetstone
(Tune: "London Bridge")
Look what we can make with shapes,
Make with shapes, make with shapes.
Look what we can make with shapes:
Something special.

Children's Books

*Captain Invincible and
the Space Shapes* by
Stuart J. Murphy
Shape by
Henry Arthur Pluckrose
Shape Space by
Cathryn Falwell

ASSESSMENT

To assess the children's learning, consider the following:
● Can the child correctly identify a circle, square, and triangle?
● Can the child use the materials to make a shape creature?

Cassandra Reigel Whetstone, Folsom, CA

Be a Shape!

5+

LEARNING OBJECTIVES

The children will:

1. Learn about basic shapes and colors.
2. Develop their ability to classify.

Materials

sentence strips
foam or
   construction
   paper of various
   colors
scissors (adult only)
stapler (adult only)

VOCABULARY

classify   group   headband   shape names

PREPARATION

- Cut differently colored shapes out of foam or construction paper.
- Staple individual shapes to the centers of the sentence strips. Laminate.
- Wrap the sentence strips in circles, and staple them to make headbands.
- Write the shape names on the shapes to enhance the children's literacy and pre-reading skills.

WHAT TO DO

1. Show the children the headbands, and engage them in a discussion about the shapes on each headband.
2. Give each child a headband to put on, and ask the children to identify the shapes they are wearing.
3. Divide the children into groups. Sing the following song with the children, encouraging them to come to the front of the classroom and stay there when they hear the name of the shape or color in their headbands.

   Circles, Circles by Shelley Hoster
   (Tune: "My Bonnie Lies Over the Ocean")
   I'm looking for all the circles.　　　*Circles, circles, come make a group*
   I'm looking for all that I see.　　　　*with me, with me.*
   I'm looking for all the circles　　　　*Circles, circles, come make a group*
   To make a group with me.　　　　　*with me!*

4. Repeat the song, substituting another shape name. Do this until all of the children are in shape groups at the front of the room.

ASSESSMENT

To assess the children's learning, consider the following:

- Can the children name the different colors and shapes on the headbands?
- Can the children classify objects in the classroom by color and shape?

Children's Books

The Circle Sarah Drew
   by Peter &
   Susan Barrett
Round Is a Pancake by
   Joan Sullivan
The Shape of Things by
   Tana Hoban

Shelley Hoster, Norcross, GA

We Can Make Shapes

5+

LEARNING OBJECTIVES

The children will:
1. Learn about shapes as they work together to create them.
2. Learn math concepts as they examine the making of shapes.
3. Learn to cooperate to create shapes.

Materials

A very long piece
of string or
ribbon
scissors (adult only)

VOCABULARY

circle	infinity	square
heptagon	octagon	together
hexagon	pentagon	triangle

WHAT TO DO

1. Cut a very long piece of string or ribbon that will be big enough for all of the children to hold in one large circle.
2. Begin with two children holding the string or ribbon between them. Ask the children, "How many ends are there?" Explain that when there are two ends, the string makes a line.
3. Ask another child to join them. Give one child both ends of the string to hold and ask the other two children to hold the string tightly with their fingers to create a triangular shape.
4. Ask the children how many sides are there now. Ask how many children are holding the string. Ask them what shape this makes.
5. Ask another child to join them by taking a part of the string and creating a new shape. Help the children form a square. Repeat the same questions.
6. Continue to add one child at a time to create a pentagon (some children may call this a house shape), a hexagon, heptagon, and octagon (which some children might call a "stop sign").

ASSESSMENT

To assess the children's learning, consider the following:
- Can the children recognize a variety of shapes?
- Can the children repeat the names of the various shapes?

Michelle Barnea, Millburn, NJ

Children's Books

Color Zoo by
Lois Ehlert
Shapes, Shapes, Shapes
by Tana Hoban
*When a Line Bends...A
Shape Begins*
by Rhonda
Gowler Greene

In the Kitchen

3+

LEARNING OBJECTIVES

The children will:

1. Identify various shapes in a kitchen setting.
2. Role-play cooking, baking, and serving and eating food.
3. Improve their vocabulary.

Materials

various kitchen
   utensils and
   cookware
colored
   construction
   paper
tape
scissors (adult only)

VOCABULARY

bake	dish	mix	pot
cook	glass	pan	spatula
cup	ladle	plate	spoon

PREPARATION

● Cut a colored paper shape to fit inside or on each kitchen item. Tape each paper shape to the item so children can clearly see the shape of each object.

WHAT TO DO

1. Display the assorted kitchen materials at the kitchen dramatic play center.
2. Invite the children to use the materials as if they were cooking, baking, serving, and eating food.
3. Help the children name each shape as they work with the tool or kitchenware.
4. Encourage the children to talk among themselves as they play.

POEM

Shapes in the Kitchen by Mary J. Murray

Shapes are in the kitchen
I see them here and there.
Shapes are in the kitchen
I see them everywhere.

I see a bowl that's round.
I see a pan that's square.
I also see a rectangle.
Shapes are everywhere.

ASSESSMENT

To assess the children's learning, consider the following:

● Can each child identify and explain how to use various kitchen utensils?
● Given a kitchen utensil, can each child explain how to use the object?
● Invite a small group of children to sort the collection of kitchen items by shape or size. Listen and assess the children's understanding of shapes and size.

Mary J. Murray, Mazomanie, WI

Children's Books

It Looked Like Spilt Milk
   by Charles Shaw
Shapes, Shapes, Shapes
   by Tana Hoban

Shape Mail

4+

LEARNING OBJECTIVES

The children will:
1. Develop their language skills.
2. Match like shapes.

Materials

6 small shoeboxes
large number of
    colored paper
    shapes
rubber stamp and
    stamp pad or
    stickers
brown purse or
    bag
American flag
"Post Office" sign

VOCABULARY

address	mail	mailbox
envelope	mailbag	shapes

PREPARATION

- Set up a small post office in the dramatic play center. Display the flag and sign. Fill the bag or purse with paper shapes.
- Attach a large paper shape to each shoebox.
- Cut a slit in each box top so children can insert mail in the box.
- Display the shape mailboxes randomly about the room.

WHAT TO DO

1. Invite the children to use the stickers or a rubberstamp and stamp pad to "stamp" the mail before it goes in the mailbag.
2. Challenge the children to put on the mailbag, remove one shape at a time, and deliver it to the correct shape mailbox.
3. Encourage the children to work until they deliver all the shape mail.

TEACHER-TO-TEACHER TIP

- Other children can open the mailboxes and remove the mail to see if the shapes match.

ASSESSMENT

To assess the children's learning, consider the following:
- Hand a child six different pieces of shape mail. Observe the child delivering the mail to see if she can match shapes correctly.
- Fill the mailbag with pictures of objects with a variety of shapes. Invite the children to come forward one by one, pull a picture from the mailbag, and then deliver it to the correct shape mailbox.

Mary J. Murray, Mazomanie, WI

Children's Books

A Monster in the Mailbox by Sheila Gordon
Tortoise Brings the Mail by Dee Hildegard
A Visit to the Post Office by Sandra Ziegler
Would You Mail a Hippo? by Vikki Woodworth

Gone Fishing

LEARNING OBJECTIVES

The children will:
1. Improve their small motor skills.
2. Develop their knowledge of shapes.
3. Practice counting.

Materials

- long strip of white cardboard
- tape
- shapes printed onto white cardstock
- crayons
- child-safe scissors
- glue sticks
- paper clips
- small magnets
- string
- small bamboo garden canes

VOCABULARY

fishing rod   fishpond   magnet   shape names

PREPARATION

- Bend a long strip of cardboard into a circular "fishpond." Tape its ends together.
- Make fishing poles by cutting a length of string, tying and gluing it around small magnets, and tying the other end of the string to one end of the bamboo cane.
- Print the outlines of various shapes on white cardstock.

WHAT TO DO

1. Set out crayons, as well as the pieces of cardstock with the shapes drawn on them. Encourage the children to color the shapes or draw faces on them.
2. Next, help the children cut out the shapes. Encourage the children to identify the shapes as they color and cut them out.
3. While each child glues one of his shapes onto the fishpond to decorate it, slide a paper clip onto each colored shape. Older children may be able to do this independently.
4. Give each child a fishing pole and show him how he can use the magnets to pick up shapes.
5. Let the children take turns fishing out a shape until the fishpond is empty.
6. Challenge older children to count how many shapes they have altogether, then how many of each shape.

TEACHER-TO-TEACHER TIP

- A short fishing pole will be easier for the children to manipulate.

ASSESSMENT

To assess the children's learning, consider the following:
- Can the children identify all the shapes they cut out?
- Can the children sort their "fish" into shapes piles without mistakes?
- Can the children count the shapes accurately?

Children's Books

Curious George Goes Fishing by Margret Rey
Gone Fishing by Earlene R. Long
The Little Fish That Got Away by Bernadine Cook

Anne Adeney, Plymouth, England, United Kingdom

Matching Halves

LEARNING OBJECTIVES

The children will:
1. Develop visual discrimination.
2. Learn about symmetry.

Materials

images of colorful
   symmetrical
   objects
scissors (adult only)
Velcro
felt or cloth board
basket

VOCABULARY

half   match   size   whole

PREPARATION

● Gather colorful pictures of symmetrical objects such as birds, butterflies, fruits, and planets.
● Laminate the images and cut in half. Round off any sharp corners and attach Velcro or felt strips to the back of each piece.
● Prepare a felt or cloth board on which the children can match the halves.
● Place the halves in a small basket next to the board.

WHAT TO DO

1. Show the children the matched halves and discuss the idea of symmetry, as well as halves.
2. Mix up the pieces in the basket. Challenge the children to pair the matching pieces with one another on the felt board.

TEACHER-TO-TEACHER TIP

● Include pictures of objects in different sizes, for example, small, medium, and large butterflies.

ASSESSMENT

To assess the children's learning, consider the following:
● Can the children match the halves independently?

Patrick Mitchell, Urayama Yagoto, Nagoya, Japan

Children's Books

A Whale Is Not a Fish by Melvin Berger
First Book of Nature— How Living Things Grow by Dwight Kuhn

Shape Hop Along

3+

LEARNING OBJECTIVES

The children will:
1. Learn to identify basic shapes by sight.
2. Develop their large motor skills.
3. Learn the names of shapes.

Materials

construction paper
markers
scissors (adult only)
bean bags
shape cards

VOCABULARY

beanbags	heart	oval	star
circle	hop	square	triangle

PREPARATION

● Prepare Hop-Along Cards on 8½" x 11" construction paper. Attach construction paper cutouts of shapes to the cards. Laminate for durability.

WHAT TO DO

1. Spread the Hop-Along Cards in a circle on the floor, in order of the number of sides they have.
2. Introduce the shapes to the children.
3. Ask the children to take turns tossing the beanbag onto one of the cards on the floor, and then identifying the shape on the card. Help the children by describing the shape, the number of sides it has, and so on.
4. Invite the child to hop to that card, counting the number of shapes he hops along to get to the beanbag.
5. Invite the children to take turns repeating the process.

TEACHER-TO-TEACHER TIP

● This is a great activity to do indoors during on a rainy day.

ASSESSMENT

To assess the children's learning, consider the following:
● Can the child recognize shapes by sight and name them?
● Can the child count the number of shapes he hops along while retrieving the beanbag?

Jason Verdone, Woodbury, NJ

Children's Books

Circus by Lois Ehrlet
Changes, Changes by Pat Hutchins
Triangle, Square, Circle by William Wegman

Felt Shapes

4+

LEARNING OBJECTIVES

The children will:
1. Learn to identify shapes.
2. Learn to look for details.

several sheets of
    different colored
    felt
marker
scissors (adult only)
construction paper

VOCABULARY

circles   difference   ovals   squares

PREPARATION

● Draw shapes (ovals, circles, rectangles, and squares) onto the felt and cut them out.
● On construction paper, write the names of the shapes you drew on the felt and then cut out the names.

WHAT TO DO

1. Engage the children in a discussion about shapes. Challenge the children to point out differences between the various shapes they know.
2. Ask the children to look around the room and identify various shapes they see.
3. Lay out the felt shape cutouts on the floor around the room. Give each child a cutout of the shape names, and challenge the children to walk to the correct shape cutout and stand on it.
4. After the children find their shapes, challenge them to take their shape name cutouts to objects in the room that have the same shape as well.

ASSESSMENT

To assess the children's learning, consider the following:
● Can the child identify the characteristic of shapes?
● Can the child accurately point to and identify various shapes around the room?
● Can the child identify the shape name card he is holding and connect the name with an object in the room that has the same shape?

Hilary Romig, Las Cruces, NM

Children's Books

Bear in a Square by Stella Blackstone
Spookley's Colorful Pumpkin Patch by Joe Troiano

Finding Shapes

4+

LEARNING OBJECTIVES

The children will:
1. Find familiar shapes in common objects.
2. Learn the names of various shapes.
3. Become more familiar with the names of objects in the classroom.

Materials

shapes cut out of paper
a bowl or bag

VOCABULARY

arrow	diamond	match	square
circle	flower	oval	star
describe	heart	rectangle	triangle

WHAT TO DO

1. Place the shape cutouts in a bag.
2. Have each child pull one shape out of the bag. Encourage him to talk about the shape.
3. Have the children find an object in the room that matches their shape. If it is a small group, the children can take individual turns. For larger groups, have two to four children look for a match to their shape at a time.
4. Encourage each child to talk about his shape and the matching object he found in the room. Some children may need assistance at first until they practice a couple of times. They may not recall the name of the shape and just make the match.
5. After the children name the objects they found, repeat the process, giving all the children new shapes to look for.

TEACHER-TO-TEACHER TIP

● To make the shapes more sturdy and reusable, cover them with clear contact paper or laminate the shapes.

ASSESSMENT

To assess the children's learning, consider the following:
● Can the child name the shape he has to find?
● Can the child name the object that matches his shape?

Sandie Nagel, White Lake, MI

Children's Books

The Shape of Things by Illustrator by Julie Lacome
Shapes, Shapes, Shapes by Tana Hoban
Who Took the Cookie from the Cookie Jar? by David Carter

Hoop Shapes Game

4+

LEARNING OBJECTIVES

The children will:
1. Develop their large motor skills.
2. Practice waiting and taking turns.
3. Identify specified shapes.

Materials

hula hoops
construction paper
scissors (adult only)

VOCABULARY

hula hoop   shape names

PREPARATION

● Cut the construction paper into a variety of shapes, so that there is one shape for every hula hoop.
● Clear a large area in the room. Set the hula hoops on the floor so the children can get to them and use them safely.

WHAT TO DO

1. Place three or more hula hoops on the floor at one end of the room.
2. Place a paper shape on the floor inside each hula hoop but keep the shape hidden from the children.
3. At the other end of the room, ask the children to sit on the floor, awaiting instructions.
4. Explain that you will call out a shape name, a type of movement, as well as the names of one to three children. The children you name get up and run to the hoop that contains the correct shape, but they must use whatever kind of movement you name. It may be hopping, crawling, walking sideways or backwards—whatever you decide will be fun and safe for the children.
5. The goal is for the children to reach the hoop containing the specified shape; it is not a race. Encourage all the children you name to stand together inside the hula hoop. Change the shapes or the number of hula hoops to keep the interest high.

TEACHER-TO-TEACHER TIP

● Consider doing this activity outside. If you do so, cut the shapes from heavier material, such as wood scraps, to prevent them from blowing away.

Children's Books

Shapes, Shapes, Shapes
by Tana Hoban
When a Line Bends…A Shape Begins by Rhonda Gowler Greene

ASSESSMENT

To assess the children's learning, consider the following:
● Can the child move to the correct hula hoop?
● Can the child move in the correct motion?

Kay Flowers, Summerfield, OH

Ice Cream Cone Race

4+

LEARNING OBJECTIVES

The children will:

1. Develop hand-eye coordination.
2. Develop an awareness of cones and spheres.

Materials

6"–8" orange
traffic cones

6" rubber balls that
fit into the open
base of the
cones

VOCABULARY

balance	group	race	team
fit	orange	sphere	traffic cone

WHAT TO DO

1. Set out the traffic cones. Show the children how to hold the points of the cones down, like ice-cream cones.
2. Balance a ball on the open end of the cone. Talk with the children, asking them what they think the cone resembles.
3. Demonstrate for the children how to move around the classroom while holding the cone and keeping the ball steady within it.
4. Give the children time to experiment holding and carrying the cones and balls.
5. Line the children up in groups of four. Give a cone and ball to the first child in each line. Challenge the children to walk the length of the room and back without dropping the ball out of the cone, and then hand the cone to the next child in line. If the children drop the ball, simply ask them to pick it up and put it back in the cone.
6. Repeat the process until all the children finish walking the length of the room with the cone.

TEACHER-TO-TEACHER TIP

- For an additional challenge, consider creating an obstacle course or non-linear racetrack to move through, or have the children pass a single ball from cone to cone.

ASSESSMENT

To assess the children's learning, consider the following.

- Can the children fit the cones and balls together?
- Can the children move around the classroom with agility and concentration?

Children's Books

Mouse Shapes by
Ellen Stoll Walsh
*The Shape of Me and
Other Stuff* by Dr. Seuss
Today Is Monday by
Eric Carle
*The Very Hungry
Caterpillar* by Eric Carle

Patrick Mitchell, Yagoto, Nagoya, Japan

Match the Shape Can

LEARNING OBJECTIVES

The children will:

1. Learn about some basic shapes.
2. Match corresponding shapes.
3. Utilize their sensory awareness.

Materials

different materials
  with texture:
  sandpaper, felt,
  bubble wrap,
  aluminum foil,
  burlap
coffee can or
  oatmeal
  container
scissors (adult only)
large poster board
colored paper
marker

VOCABULARY

bumpy	match	shiny
circle	rectangle	smooth
heart	rough	triangle

PREPARATION

● Cover a can or oatmeal container with brightly colored paper.
● Cut out various shapes from the differently textured materials.
● Trace the cutout shapes onto a large piece of poster board, making a matching game mat.
● Laminate the game mat for durability. Consider mounting the textured shape cutouts on poster board for durability.

WHAT TO DO

1. Show the children all the differently textured shape cutouts you prepared.
2. Identify the shapes for the children and discuss the characteristics of each. Also, match the shape cutout to the like shape on the game mat, so the children can see how they match.
3. After introducing each shape to the children, put it into the can.
4. When all the shapes are in the can, have the children take turns pulling shape cutouts out of the can and matching them to the corresponding shape outlines on the game mat.

TEACHER-TO-TEACHER TIP

● Consider making a "big" version of this game, putting very large cutouts in a large bin and drawing their outlines on a large sheet or shower curtain.

ASSESSMENT

To assess the children's learning, consider the following:
● Can the children match the shapes to their outlines on the game mat?
● Can the children identify basic shapes by sight and feel?

Jason Verdone, Woodbury, NJ

Children's Books

Changes, Changes by
Pat Hutchins
Circus by Lois Ehlert

Pass the Shapes

LEARNING OBJECTIVES

The children will:

1. Identify a variety of shapes by name.
2. Match like shapes.
3. Cooperate with one another.

Materials

music
6 colorful tag
board shapes;
circle, triangle,
square,
rectangle, oval,
diamond.
bold marker

VOCABULARY

alike	match	similar
identify	shapes	two

PREPARATION

● Set out pictures or objects of all six shapes (circle, square, triangle, rectangle, diamond, and oval).

● Use a bold marker to draw a smiley face on both sides of the tag board circle.

WHAT TO DO

1. Invite the children to sit in a circle.
2. Hand the six paper shapes to six children, evenly spaced about the circle.
3. Explain that when the music starts, the children are to pass the shapes around the circle.
4. After a few moments, stop the music. The children who are holding shapes should carry those shapes to an object in the room with a similar shape. Encourage the children to verbalize their comparisons, using a sentence such as "The doorknob is round, like this circle," and "The book is a rectangle."
5. Explain that whoever ends up with the smiley face circle has to walk around the circle and give a high five to all the children before sitting back down.
6. After the children return to their places on the floor, continue the game until everyone has had several chances to identify shapes in the classroom, or until the children are finished playing the game.

ASSESSMENT

To assess the children's learning, consider the following:

● Can the children correctly match the shapes?

● Display the six shapes and a bucket of shape objects. Can small groups of children sort the shape objects onto the large paper shapes?

● Invite groups of children to lie on the floor and use their bodies together to create shapes.

Children's Books

Round Is a Mooncake
by Roseanne Thong
Shapes by
Chuck Murphy

Mary J. Murray, Mazomanie, WI

Reading and Matching Shape Word Cards

4+

Materials

white paper
scissors (adult only)
marker

LEARNING OBJECTIVES

The children will:
1. Begin to learn how to read the names of shapes.
2. Match written shape names to images of shapes.

VOCABULARY

circle	game	oval	star
crescent	heart	rectangle	teardrop
diamond	match	square	triangle

PREPARATION

● Make a set of white cards approximately 3" x 4" in size.
● Write the name of one of the 10 shapes on each card and laminate.
● Draw the 10 shapes whose names you wrote on the first 10 cards on the 10 remaining cards.

WHAT TO DO

1. Display a Shape Card and ask the children to name the shape on the card.
2. Show the matching Word Card and help the children identify the word. Initially, it is better to play with a few cards.
3. Encourage the children to play matching games on the floor, table, or whiteboard. For example, line the Shape Cards up on the whiteboard and hand a child a Word Card. Help him read it if necessary. Then help the child place the Word Card under the corresponding Shape Card.
4. To make it a language game, give each child a Shape Card or a Word Card. The task is to find a matching shape by asking and answering, "What shape do you have?" "I have a square."

TEACHER-TO-TEACHER TIP

● For an advanced challenge, place the Word Cards or Shape Cards on the whiteboard and have the children write the shape names under the cards with a whiteboard marker.

Children's Books

I Like Shapes by Shane Armstrong and Celina Mosbauer
Triangles by Marybeth Lorbiecker

ASSESSMENT

To assess the children's learning, consider the following:
● Can the children match a shape to its name?
● Are the children beginning to learn how to spell the names of shapes?

Patrick Mitchell, Yagoto, Nagoya, Japan

Shape Sssssnake Relay

4+

LEARNING OBJECTIVES

The children will:

1. Recognize similar shapes.
2. Improve their oral language skills.
3. Improve their critical-thinking skills.
4. Practice counting.

Materials

40 6" paper
   shapes, 10 of
   each shape
   (circles, squares,
   triangles,
   rectangles)
4 6' lengths of yarn
maraca

VOCABULARY

count	long	match	shapes
how	many	number	snake

PREPARATION

- Draw a face on one of each shape to represent each snake's head.
- Hide or display the remaining paper shapes at the children's level around the room.

WHAT TO DO

1. Place the four snakehead shapes on the floor. Display the maraca on a table.
2. Place a length of string behind each snakehead, extending outward.
3. Divide the children into four groups and have each group sit near a snakehead.
4. On the command of "Ready, set, find your snake," invite the groups to search around the classroom to find the matching shape pieces to create their snake's bodies. Each group will find nine shapes.
5. As each child finds a shape, he brings it back to the snake and places it along the length of yarn, creating the shape snake.
6. When a snake has all 10 shapes, one child in the group shakes the maraca, signaling that his group's snake is complete.

TEACHER-TO-TEACHER TIP

- Invite the children to find an assortment of different shapes to create their snake. Have children identify the various shapes as they put the snake together.

ASSESSMENT

To assess the children's learning, consider the following:

- Can the children identify each shape on their snake?
- Can the children work with each other to complete a task?

Children's Books

Mouse Count by
Ellen Stoll Walsh
See a Circle by
Ben Mahan
What's That Sound? by
Lisa Ann Marsoli

Mary J. Murray, Mazomanie, WI

Spin-a-Shape

4+

LEARNING OBJECTIVES

The children will:

1. Recognize and identify various shapes.
2. Identify colors by name.
3. Develop their small motor skills.
4. Follow sequential directions.

Materials

board game
   spinner cards
colored markers or
   construction
   paper
scissors (adult only)
brass fastener

VOCABULARY

cooperation	diamond	rectangle	spinner
cube	oval	sphere	square

PREPARATION

- Divide the card into equal segments, similar to a pie-graph circle.
- Draw or glue shapes and colors within the drawn segments on the card.
- Use a brass fastener to attach a board game spinner or cutout arrow shape to the center of the circle.

WHAT TO DO

1. With the children, review the names of the shapes and colors on the Spin-a-Shape card.
2. Explain to the children that they will take turns spinning the spinner and naming the shape and/or color to which the arrow points.
3. Invite the children to work with partners with one child spinning the spinner and the other identifying the shapes.
4. Challenge the children to identify objects in the classroom that are similar colors or have similar shapes to those on the Spin-a-Shape card.

FINGERPLAY

Shapes Around Us by Margery Kranyik Fermino

Point to a circle,

Point to a square,

Point to a triangle,

Shapes are everywhere!

Point to a rectangle,

And another square,

Point to an oval,

Shapes are everywhere!

ASSESSMENT

To assess the children's learning, consider the following:

- Were the children able to operate the spinner and follow directions?
- Did the children correctly identify the shapes and colors?
- Were children able to connect the shapes on the spinner to the shapes of the objects in the classroom?

Children's Books

My Very First Book of Shapes by Eric Carle
The Greedy Triangle by Marilyn Burns

Margery Kranyik Fermino, West Roxbury, MA

Scavenger Hunt

LEARNING OBJECTIVES

The children will:
1. Identify shapes.
2. Find each shape's three-dimensional equivalent in ordinary objects.

Materials

chalkboard
chalk
objects with
    definite shapes
    (or pictures of
    them), at least
    one of every
    shape per child
bags
pencils/crayons

VOCABULARY

circle	oval	square	triangle
cylinder	rectangle	three-dimensional	

PREPARATION

- Create a list with six to eight shapes drawn on it, one per child (or group).
- Prepare at least six stations with various items at each station.
- Give each child (or group) a list, a pencil, and a bag.

WHAT TO DO

1. Draw different shapes on the chalkboard and challenge the children to name each one. Explain that every object in the world is made of different shapes. Identify one or two shapes in the room to demonstrate this. Encourage your children to spot a few as well.
2. Tell the children that they will participate in a scavenger hunt. Show them the list of shapes and the stations around the room. Their job is to visit each station and to collect objects that resemble the shapes depicted on their lists.
3. Explain to the children that once they find an object that matches a shape on their list, they should put it into their bag and cross that shape off their list. The children continue searching until they find an object for every shape.

TEACHER-TO-TEACHER TIPS

- For an advanced challenge, let the children discover shapes found outside (for example, squares in hopscotch, rectangles on doors, and triangles in a sidewalk).
- Consider challenging the children to see who can spot the most shapes or the most creative shapes (trapezoids, pyramids, diamonds, and so on).

ASSESSMENT

To assess the children's learning, consider the following:
- Can the children find objects that match the shapes on their lists?
- As a class, or in smaller groups, ask the children to identify and discuss one or two of the objects they collected.

Children's Books

I Spy Shapes in Art by Lucy Micklethwait
Mouse Shapes by Ellen Stoll Walsh

Angela Hawkins, Denver, CO

Shapes Bingo

5+

LEARNING OBJECTIVES

The children will:
1. Improve levels of concentration.
2. Improve their listening skills.

Materials

bingo shape card
for each child
with four
different shapes
on each, plus
second card cut
into four
quarters
set of nine
different shape
cards
scissors (adult only)

VOCABULARY

bingo	moon	rectangle	triangle
circle	oval	semi-circle	
diamond	play	square	
game	quarter	star	

PREPARATION

- Use a thick marker to divide blank cardstock into four quarters. Pass out two divided cards to each child.
- Find or make pictures of shapes: square, circle, triangle, rectangle, diamond, semi-circle, oval, star, moon, and so on. Put up the shape pictures where all the children can see them.

WHAT TO DO

1. Tell the children that they are going to make their own boards for a game of shape bingo.
2. Ask the children to choose four different shapes and then help the children draw one of those shapes in each quarter of their papers. Help the children cut a second sheet of cardstock into four blank pieces. These will cover the shapes on their bingo cards.
3. Show the children the different shape pictures. Encourage the children to identify each shape and see if they can match the shapes to those on their bingo cards.
4. If a child has that shape on his bingo card, he should cover the shape with one of the blank pieces of cardstock. The first child to cover his board is the winner and can shout "Bingo!"

Children's Books

Bingo! by
Rosemary Wells
Shape Spotters by
Megan E. Bryant
*Three Pigs, One Wolf,
Seven Magic Shapes* by
Grace Maccarone

ASSESSMENT

To assess the children's learning, consider the following:
- Can the children name all the shapes?
- Can the children draw the shapes or do they need templates?
- Can the children follow the rules of the game?

Anne Adeney, Plymouth, England, United Kingdom

Shape Cards

3+

LEARNING OBJECTIVES

The children will:

1. Identify basic shapes.
2. Reinforce an understanding of the pattern of question-and-answer discussions.

Materials

brightly colored
construction
paper
scissors (adult only)
markers

VOCABULARY

circle	oval	rectangle	star
crescent	diamond	square	triangle

PREPARATION

● Cut brightly colored construction paper into the shapes in the vocabulary list.
● Make each shape a different color and approximately 5" x 5".
● Write the name of the shape on the card.
● Laminate and round any sharp corners.

WHAT TO DO

1. Show each shape card to the children and have them repeat the name of each shape.
2. Place the cards on the floor or table and encourage the children to race to pick up the card as you name it. Also consider placing the cards in a line along a wall and having the children run to retrieve the appropriate cards.
3. For a language exercise, display the cards and ask a child, "What shape do you like?" The child picks a card and describes it, saying, for instance, "I like hearts. How about you?"
4. For an art activity, show the children how to place the cards under thin paper and trace the shapes in pencil. They can then color or decorate their shapes.

TEACHER-TO-TEACHER TIP

● You can also back these versatile cards with self-adhesive magnetic strips so that they stick on a cookie sheet or whiteboard.

ASSESSMENT

To assess the children's learning, consider the following:

● Are the children learning about ovals, crescents, and drops as well as basic shapes?
● How engaged were the children during the exchange about the shape?

Patrick Mitchell, Yagoto, Nagoya, Japan

Children's Books

I Am Water by
Jean Marzollo
*Papa, Please Get the
Moon for Me* by
Eric Carle

Classroom Triangle Book 4+

LEARNING OBJECTIVES

The children will:
1. Learn to notice triangles in the everyday world.
2. Develop their large motor skills.

Materials

9" x 12" construction paper in yellow
scissors (adult only)
crayons and markers
construction paper triangles in a variety of sizes and colors
glue sticks
hole punch
yarn

VOCABULARY

book	triangle	yellow
bound	yarn	

PREPARATION

- Cut the yellow construction paper into triangles. Make a triangle with a 12" base.
- Cut construction paper triangles in a variety of sizes and colors, some equilateral and some in the shapes of pennants.

WHAT TO DO

1. Engage the children in a discussion about triangles in the everyday world. Challenge them to find triangles in the classroom.
2. Encourage the children to think of triangles outside of the classroom. Help them come up with a list of triangles they might find in the world.
3. Give each child a yellow triangle. Ask them to pick a triangle-shaped object they would like to draw.
4. Help the children glue the triangles onto sheets of construction paper, and then encourage them to use markers to fill in the details on their triangle-shaped objects.
5. When the children complete their triangle pictures, ask them to describe what the triangles in their pictures are doing. Copy their descriptions onto their pages.
6. Punch holes along the 12" side of the children's pages and use rings or yarn to bind the book. Read it aloud to the children.

Children's Books

Circles, Triangles, and Squares by Tana Hoban
The Greedy Triangle by Marilyn Burns
My Very First Book of Shapes by Eric Carle
Shape, Shape by Cathryn Falwell

ASSESSMENT

To assess the children's learning, consider the following:
- Did the children identify triangle-shaped objects to draw?
- Did the children glue the triangles onto the paper successfully?

Susan Oldham Hill, Lakeland, FL

Inside the Circle

4+

LEARNING OBJECTIVES

The children will:

1. Learn the name of the shape circle.
2. Identify when objects are inside a circle, thereby reinforcing an understanding of the boundaries, in this case of the shape of a circle.

Materials

10" inner circle of embroidery hoops (1 per child)

variety of small classroom items

VOCABULARLY

circle	embroidery	outside
curved	hoop	round
edge	inside	smooth

WHAT TO DO

1. Give each child an embroidery hoop.
2. Encourage the children to run their fingers along the edge. Talk about its features, including how smooth, round, or curved it is.
3. Encourage children to say the word "circle" aloud.
4. Describe how the circle has an "inside." Set it on the floor and put objects inside the circle. Also place objects outside the circle for comparison.
5. Invite the children to put objects inside the circle.
6. Examine objects inside the hoops with the children.

ASSESSMENT

To assess the children's learning, consider the following:

- Can the children name the shape of the embroidery hoop?
- When given a variety of objects, can the children correctly discriminate between circular items and non-circular items?

Karyn F. Everham, Fort Myers, FL

Children's Books

In Out by Richard Duerrstein
Snake In, Snake Out by Linda Banchek
What's Inside? by Duanne Daughtry

Mirror on the Wall

4+

LEARNING OBJECTIVES

The children will:

1. Improve their language skills.
2. Gain self-confidence.
3. Identify shapes and their attributes.

Materials

four different
 plastic shapes;
 circle, square,
 rectangle,
 triangle
chair
small basket

VOCABULARY

color	describe	mirror	sides
corner	me	shapes	

PREPARATION

- Hang or display a large mirror on a wall in the classroom.
- Arrange a chair so that it faces the mirror and is 1'–2' away from the mirror.
- Place the shapes in the basket and place it on the floor between the mirror and the chair.

WHAT TO DO

1. Ask one child to sit in the chair facing the mirror and hold the basket on her lap.
2. Encourage the child to remove a shape from the basket and identify it.
3. Invite the child to talk about the shape as she holds it in her hands, feeling the various corners and sides. Have the child to look in the mirror as she speaks.
4. Have the child repeat the activity for each shape in the basket.

POEM

Shapes and Me by Mary J. Murray
I like shapes,
And I like me.
Pick up a shape.
Tell what you see.

Children's Books

Shapes by
Henry Arthur Pluckrose
Shapes, a Book by
John Reiss
*The Brambleberry's
Animal Book of Big and
Small Shapes* by
Marianna Mayer

ASSESSMENT

To assess the children's learning, consider the following:

- Can the child identify the shapes she pulls from the basket?
- Can the child describe one shape in contrast to other shapes?

Mary J. Murray, Mazomanie, WI

My Shape Book

4+

LEARNING OBJECTIVES

The children will:

1. Develop their small motor skills.
2. Create a book of shapes they can share with younger children.

VOCABULARY

circle	rectangle	shapes	triangle
oval	recycled paper	square	

PREPARATION

- Fold sheets of paper in half.
- Place three sheets inside one cover page to make a book and staple it together.
- Write a shape word on the top of each inside blank page: circle, square, and triangle, then paste cutout images of those shapes on the corresponding pages.

WHAT TO DO

1. Talk with the children about various shapes.
2. Show the children a sample shape book, with shapes pasted on each page. Explain that they will each be making their own books.
3. Give each child a blank book and challenge them to search old magazines and newspapers for shape pictures.
4. Help the children cut out the pictures and glue them to the appropriate page.
5. After the children finish pasting shapes into their books, help them write book titles on the covers, such as *My Shape Book* or *Abby's Shape Book*.
6. Keep the books in the class library for the children to look through.

TEACHER-TO-TEACHER TIP

- If time is a factor, cut out pictures before the children do the project. Alternatively, ask the children to bring in a number of pictures they cut out at home.

ASSESSMENT

To assess the children's learning, consider the following:

- Can the children recognize shapes in everyday objects?
- Are the children able to paste shapes on the appropriate pages?
- Do the children indicate that they understand how books are made?

Donna Alice Patton, Hillsboro, OH

Materials

4 sheets of 8½" x 11" white paper per child
markers, crayons, or colored pencils
old magazines, newspapers, or junk mail
glue sticks
child-safe scissors
stapler (adult only)

Children's Books

Ovals by Julia Vogel
Rectangles by Pamela Hall
Squares by Pamela Hall

Push Cars

3+

LEARNING OBJECTIVES

The children will:

1. Recognize shapes.
2. Improve their large motor and coordination skills.

Materials

4–6 large paper
   boxes
colored paper
black paper wheel
   shapes
glue
permanent marker
   (adult only)

VOCABULARY

car   push   shapes   wheel
color

PREPARATION

- Attach a sheet of colored paper to each side of each box.
- Attach four black paper wheels to each box.
- Draw the same shape on each side of each box.

WHAT TO DO

1. Display the shape cars in the classroom.
2. Encourage the children to name the shape on each car.
3. Demonstrate how to push the cars around the room.
4. Invite the children to push the cars around the room. Encourage the children to seek various objects according to the shape on their car.

5. After the children spot several objects, each child may return his car and select another car to push.

ASSESSMENT

To assess the children's learning, consider the following:

- Invite the children to line up all six cars in a row. Instruct the class to walk along the row of cars and name the shape as they pass by each one. Can the children identify the shapes?
- Invite the children to set a stuffed animal inside their car. When the car returns, invite each "animal" to talk about the shapes it saw while on the ride.

Mary J. Murray, Mazomanie, WI

Children's Books

Cars and Trucks by
   Matthew Rupert
*I Can Be a Race Car
   Driver* by Sylvia
   Wilkinson

Run the Bases

3+

LEARNING OBJECTIVES

The children will:
1. Develop their large motor skills.
2. Develop their ability to follow directions.
3. Recognize shapes.

Materials

felt shapes
four bases

VOCABULARY

bases	group	second
carry	home	shapes
first	run	third

PREPARATION

- Arrange the four bases as if setting up a baseball diamond.

WHAT TO DO

1. Provide each child with a felt shape.
2. Demonstrate how to run the bases in order.
3. Invite the children to recite "first, second, third, home run" aloud.
4. Then, call out a specific shape. For example, "Circles run the bases." At that command, all children holding a circle run the four bases carrying their circle along with them.
5. Once all of the children have returned home, direct another group of children to run the bases.
6. After all the groups have run the bases, invite the children to change shapes with a friend.
7. Repeat the activity several times.

TEACHER-TO-TEACHER TIP

- For extra fun, give each child a 2' segment of crepe paper with a shape drawn on one end. Invite the children to run with the shape streamer in the air, letting it fly as they move around the bases.

ASSESSMENT

To assess the children's learning, consider the following:
- Can each child identify his individual shape?
- Can each child identify the order of the bases?

Mary J. Murray, Mazomanie, WI

Children's Books

At the Ball Game by Sydell Kramer
Baseball Mouse by Syd Hoff
How Spider Saved the Baseball Game by Robert Kraus
Paul the Pitcher by Paul Sharp

Shape Tunnel

3+

LEARNING OBJECTIVES

The children will:

1. Learn to follow instructions.
2. Improve their memory skills.
3. Reinforce their knowledge of shapes.

Materials

large, sturdy
  cardboard
  cartons
scissors (adults
  only)
packaging tape

VOCABULARY

circular	oval	triangular
crawl	semi-circular	tunnel

PREPERATION

- Open each carton at both ends.
- Cut large openings on the opposite sides of the cartons in the shapes the children are learning.
- Attach the cartons together in a long line by taping the flaps at each end to the next box. You should now have a strong cardboard tunnel with "windows" in assorted shapes.

WHAT TO DO

1. Let the children take turns entering the tunnel and crawling out through a shape window of their choice.
2. When each of the children has done this once, see if they can remember and follow several instructions at once. For example, ask a child to "Crawl out of the diamond window, back in through the circle window, and come out."
3. With older children, increase the types of window shapes and the number of instructions to follow.
4. When the children are ready, start introducing adjectives such as *circular*, *semi-circular*, and *triangular*.

FINGERPLAY

This Is the Church (Traditional)
This is the church, (hold hands down with fingers interlocked)
This is the steeple. (put up both index fingers in the shape of a steeple)
Look inside. (children turn hands over, still with interlocked fingers)
And see all the people. (wiggle fingers to indicate people)

Children's Books

Icky Bug Shapes by Jerry
  Pallotta
Mouse Shapes by Ellen
  Stoll Walsh
*When a Line Bends . . . A
  Shape Begins* by
Rhonda Gowler Greene

ASSESSMENT

To assess the children's learning, consider the following:
- Do the children recognize the shapes in such a different context?
- Can the children recognize shapes by name?

Anne Adeney, Plymouth, England, United Kingdom

Let's Halve Fun

4+

LEARNING OBJECTIVES

The children will:
1. Develop their large motor skills.
2. Improve their understanding of what shapes and fractions are.

Materials

balance beam (low
  to the ground)
sidewalk chalk
12″ cardstock
  shapes, cut into
  halves

VOCABULARY

balance	match	symmetry	whole
half	shapes	walk	

PREPARATION

- Use sidewalk chalk to draw 12″ shapes randomly around the playground area.

WHAT TO DO

1. Invite the children to line up at one end of the balance beam.
2. Hand each child a shape half.
3. Have the children cross the balance beam, one at a time, carrying the shape piece with them.
4. Once the children step down from the beam, ask each of them to find a shape on the ground that matches their shape halves, and then set their shape halves beside the matching chalk shapes.
5. Continue the activity until all the shapes are complete with two halves.

TEACHER-TO-TEACHER TIPS

- You can play this in the classroom using paper shapes on the floor. If you don't have a balance beam, simply tape a length of masking tape to the floor for children to walk across.
- For extra fun, set a shape on the beam and see if the children can walk to the shape, pick it up, and then continue across the beam without falling off the beam.
- Consider explaining to the children that the matching halves of a shape are mirror images of one another, and that they make a symmetrical shape when you join them.

ASSESSMENT

To assess the children's learning, consider the following:
- Can the children cross the balance beam without falling off?
- Can the children divide the chalk shapes in half?
- Can the children identify the shapes, even when divided in half?

Children's Books

Eating Fractions by
Bruce McMillan
Give Me Half! by
Stuart J Murphy
*How Many Ways Can
You Cut a Pie?* by
Jane Belk Moncure

Mary J. Murray, Mazomanie, WI

People Shapes

LEARNING OBJECTIVES

The children will:
1. Learn to identify a triangle, square, and rectangle.
2. Improve their large motor skills.

Materials

set of shape flashcards for triangle, square, and rectangle.
bag

VOCABULARY

circle	identify	square
count	rectangle	triangle

WHAT TO DO

1. Place the shape flashcards in the bag.
2. Engage the children in a discussion about the number of sides for each shape.
3. Ask a child to draw a shape from the bag and count the sides.
4. Ask the child to choose some friends with whom to lie down and make the shape on the rug.
5. Pick another child and challenge him to identify the shape.
6. Let the child who identified the first shape draw the next shape out of the bag.
7. Repeat the activity. Continue until all the children have a chance to pick a shape and choose other children with whom to make it.

ASSESSMENT

To assess the children's learning, consider the following:
- Does the child choose the right number of friends to make the shape he picked from the bag?
- Can the child identify the shapes the other children make?

Susan Oldham Hill, Lakeland, FL

Children's Books

Circles, Triangles, and Squares by Tana Hoban
Frog and Toad Are Friends by Arnold Lobel
My Friends by Taro Gomi

Shape Toss

4+

LEARNING OBJECTIVES

The children will:

1. Develop their large motor skills.
2. Improve their counting skills.
3. Recognize the difference between *more than* and *less than*.

Materials

large foam shapes
(store bought or
cut from 1½"
craft foam
masking tape or
yarn

VOCABULARY

count	line	team
game	more	throw
less	shape	toss

PREPARATION

● Use yarn or masking tape to create a game line in the middle of an open area in your classroom.

WHAT TO DO

1. Invite five children to sit on each side of the center line.
2. Place an assortment of foam shapes on each side of the line.
3. On the command of "ready, set, shape toss," have the children pick up a shape, identify it, and throw it over the line onto the other team's side of the line.
4. Have the children play for several minutes.
5. Help each team count how many shapes are on their side of the line.
6. Invite 10 different children into the game area to have a shape toss.
7. Continue until each child has had several turns.

TEACHER-TO-TEACHER TIP

● An easy alternative is a circle toss. Simply have the children throw foam balls across the line.

Children's Books

Circles by
Mary Salzmann
*Circus of Shapes: Fun
with all Your Exciting
Friends at the Big Top*
by Kent Salisbury
Flip-a-Shape: Go!
by SAMi

ASSESSMENT

To assess the children's learning, consider the following:

● Can the children name each shape before they toss it?
● Can the children respect boundaries when it comes to tossing items in the air?

Mary J. Murray, Mazomanie, WI

Hidden Shapes

4+

LEARNING OBJECTIVES

The children will:

1. Become familiar with the tactile differences between squares and circles.
2. Match squares and to objects that have square-like shapes.

Materials

shoeboxes, one
    per child
cloth,
    approximately
    4" x 4", 2 per
    box
stapler (adult only)
blocks

VOCABULARY

corner(s)	pointy	same	touch
different	round	smooth	

PREPARATION

● Cut two holes into the top of each box. The holes should be large enough for the children to fit their hands through them.
● Use the pieces of cloth to create a curtain for each hole by stapling one edge of the cloth to the box top. Place one square and one circular block into each box.

WHAT TO DO

1. Give each child a box.
2. Invite the children to put one hand into each hole and without looking or taking the items out, guess what is inside. If the children limit their descriptions of the items as "blocks," encourage them to make comparisons and consider shape by asking questions such as:
    ● How do the blocks feel the same?
    ● How do they feel different?
    ● Which block feels pointy?
    ● Which block feels round?
3. Show the children round and square blocks, one at a time. Ask the children to find the matching block without looking in the box.
4. Then, ask the children to take the correct shape from the box.

ASSESSMENT

To assess the children's learning, consider the following:

● Can the children describe the differences between the blocks?
● Can the children match the blocks?

Karyn F. Everham, Fort Myers, FL

Children's Books

Shapes by
Henry Arthur Pluckrose
Shapes: A Book by
John Reiss
Shapes and Things by
Tana Hoban

Songs

"Circle Song" by
Harry Chapin
"Ring Around the
Rosy" (Traditional)

Shapes in a Shape

4+

LEARNING OBJECTIVES

The children will:
1. Identify shapes.
2. Match shapes with everyday objects.

Materials

paper
magazines (or clip art)
child-safe scissors (optional)
glue

VOCABULARY

abstract   match   outline

PREPARATION

● Create a packet for each child with several shapes drawn on paper. If appropriate, cut out pictures for the children.

WHAT TO DO

1. Show the children each shape in the packet and help them identify each one. Explain that shapes are found everywhere. Hold up a few items and help the children match the object with its shape

2. Explain to the children that they will also be matching objects to their shapes. Encourage the children to look through magazines to locate and cut out shape pictures (or they can sort through the pictures you have cut out).

3. After they find enough pictures, have the children sort through and pair and glue each picture with its matching shape in the packet.

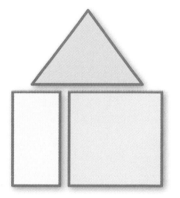

TEACHER-TO-TEACHER TIP

● Some shapes will obviously be trickier to find. Let the children know that they can circle something within a picture.

ASSESSMENT

To assess the children's learning, consider the following:
● Is the child finding images of objects that match the shape outline she has?
● How well is the child describing the matching object she found?

Angela Hawkins, Denver, CO

Children's Books

Eye Like Shapes & Patterns by Play Bac
When a Line Bends…A Shape Begins by Rhonda Gowler Greene

The Magic Snake

3+

LEARNING OBJECTIVES

The children will:

1. Identify four basic shapes.
2. Alternate their feet as they walk along the path of the snake.
3. Take turns cooperating with their classmates.

Materials

chalk
washable paint

VOCABULARY

diamond	identify	shapes	walk
hexagon	octagon	star	

PREPARATION

- With chalk or washable paint, draw two very large and long snakes, at least 12" wide, which resemble winding paths from the head to the tail of the snake.
- Inside one snake, draw the four basic shapes about 10" in diameter and about 5" apart, until you fill the snake. Leave the second snake's shape blank.

WHAT TO DO

1. Ask the children to start at the head of the snake and walk along the path of the outlined snake, identifying the shapes as they step from one to the other.
2. Start with the four basic shapes and then add different shapes later.
3. Challenge the children to identify the number of sides each shape has as they step from shape to shape within the snake.
4. After the children are familiar with the process of the activity, give the children pieces of chalk and challenge the each child to draw a specific shape within the second snake. Help the children as necessary.
5. When the children finish filling in the second shape snake, invite them to walk through it, as they did the first snake.

ASSESSMENT

To assess the children's learning, consider the following:

- Can the child identify the shapes within the first snake?
- Can the child copy the appropriate shape inside the second snake?

Judy Fujawa, The Villages, FL

Children's Books

Pancakes, Crackers, and Pizza: A Book of Shapes by Marjorie Eberts
Shapes by Robert Crowther

Match the Shape

3+

LEARNING OBJECTIVES

The children will:
1. Identify four basic shapes.
2. Match cardboard shapes to the shapes outlined on the blacktop.
3. Begin to match shapes more quickly over time.

Materials

cardboard shapes
scissors (adult only)
chalk

VOCABULARY

circle   match   rectangle   square

PREPARATION

- Cut out four circles, four squares, four triangles, and four rectangles. The shapes should be 8" x 10" across.
- Use chalk to trace outlines of the shapes on the pavement.
- Trace three of each shape on the pavement in random order.

WHAT TO DO

1. Distribute the cardboard shapes to the children. Talk with the children about the number of sides they see on each shape.
2. Challenge the children to match the shapes to the correct outlines on the pavement. Set no time limit when the children start.
3. After a while, start timing how long it takes the children to match all of the shapes. Do this activity as a group or one child at a time.

TEACHER-TO-TEACHER TIP

- Be enthusiastic and complimentary as the children match the shapes. Encourage cooperative behavior. Invite shy children to participate, and give all the children an opportunity to "share and show" their ideas.

ASSESSMENT

To assess the children's learning, consider the following:
- Can the child differentiate between the number of sides the various shapes have?
- Can the child consistently match the shape outlines on the ground to the correct cutouts?

Children's Books

Is it Larger? Is it Smaller? by Tana Hoban
Shapes, Shapes, Shapes by Tana Hoban

Judy Fujawa, The Villages, FL

Sort the Squares

3+

LEARNING OBJECTIVES

The children will:

1. Identify squares.
2. Examine an assortment of shapes and sort out the squares.

Materials

10–12 felt shapes,
   including
   squares, circles,
   triangles, and
   ovals
square box
piece of
   construction
   paper

VOCABULARY

circle	sides	square
oval	sort	triangle

WHAT TO DO

1. Place one felt shape in front of each child. Talk with the children about the different shapes they see in front of them.
2. Talk with the children about the number of sides on a square.
3. Ask the children who have squares in front of them to hold them up. Help children as needed.
4. Explain to the children that all of the square shapes belong in the square box, and all of the other shapes belong on the piece of construction paper.
5. Invite each child to sort the shapes into their proper places.

TEACHER-TO-TEACHER TIP

- Cut all of the shapes from the same color felt so that the children can focus on sorting shapes, not colors.

SONG

Every Square by Laura Wynkoop
(Tune: "London Bridge")
Every square has just four sides,
Just four sides, just four sides.
Every square has just four sides,
Count them and you'll see.

Children's Books

What Is a Square? by
Rebecca Kai Dotlich
Bear in a Square by
Stella Blackstone

ASSESSMENT

To assess the children's learning, consider the following:

- Given an assortment of felt shapes, can the children sort out the squares?
- Can the children identify other square objects in the room?

Laura Wynkoop, San Dimas, CA

Animal Dance

4+

LEARNING OBJECTIVES

The children will:
1. Identify four basic shapes.
2. Improve their listening skills.

Materials

collection of
  beanbag toy
  animals
paper shape mats
  (one for each
  child)

VOCABULARY

animal	jump	shapes
hop	lay	sit

PREPARATION

● Create a shape mat as follows: Draw a circle, square, triangle, and rectangle on a sheet of paper, filling the page with the four shapes. Make one copy of the mat for each child.

WHAT TO DO

1. Give each child a beanbag animal and a shape mat.
2. Ask the children to place their animals next to their mats.
3. Give specific directions to the children, such as "Make your animal sit on the circle," "Help your animal hop on the square," "Make your animal lie across the rectangle," or "Help your animal dance on the triangle."
4. After giving the children several directions for what to do with their animals, challenge the children to take turns calling out specific direction shapes for the animals to follow.
5. Play until the animals have moved several times on the different shapes.

TEACHER-TO-TEACHER TIP

● Always keep a collection of beanbag toy animals on hand. Use them for spur of the moment activities.

Children's Books

Bear in a Square by Stella Blackstone
Listen to a Shape by Marcia Brown-nature *Shapes* by Tony Ross

ASSESSMENT

To assess the children's learning, consider the following:
● Can the children place their beanbag animals on the correct shapes?
● Take note of which children may need to improve their listening or shape-recognition skills and work with these children at a later time.

Mary J. Murray, Mazomanie, WI

Matching Circles

4+

LEARNING OBJECTIVES

The children will:
1. Match circular shapes by size.
2. Count the objects used.

Materials

jar tops of various
    sizes
basket
poster board
clear, adhesive-
    backed contact
    paper
permanent black
    marker (adult
    only)

VOCABULARY

circles   equal   jar top   match
count

PREPARATION

- Using a permanent black marker, trace the jar tops onto the poster board, leaving a little space between each one.
- Cover the board with contact paper to protect it.

WHAT TO DO

1. Show the children the various jar tops, as well as their outlines on the poster board.
2. With the children, count the number of jar tops and circles. Talk with the children about how the number of each is equal, and how this is an example of one-to-one correspondence.
3. Invite the children match the jar tops to their outlines on the poster board.
4. Challenge the children to arrange the jar tops in a row or atop one another in ascending or descending order.

TEACHER-TO-TEACHER TIP

- Make boards for other shapes, using small boxes (squares or rectangles) or triangles, ovals, or other shapes cut from cardboard. Increase the difficulty by creating a board with a mixture of shapes.

ASSESSMENT

To assess the children's learning, consider the following:
- Can the child match the jar tops to their outlines?
- Can the child place the jar tops in order from largest to smallest?

Mary Jo Shannon, Roanoke, VA

Children's Books

A Circle Here, a Square There: My Shapes Book by David Diehl
Circles by Jon Kottk

Math Matching Game

4+

LEARNING OBJECTIVES

The children will:
1. Match two puzzle pieces.
2. Match number shapes to proper tactile amounts.

Materials

poster board or
   thin cardboard
felt
glue, if floor
   protectors are
   not already
   gummed
scissors (adult only)
thick permanent
   marker

VOCABULARY

count   puzzle   shapes   tactile
match

PREPARATION

- Cut poster board or thin cardboard into 5" x 7" pieces of various shapes.
- Cut several smaller matching shapes out of the felt.
- On half of each 5" x 7" shape, write a large numeral from 1–10.
- On the other half of the shape, glue a matching number felt circles.
- Cut a wavy or zigzag line through the middle of each card to make a simple, two-piece puzzle.

WHAT TO DO

1. Mix up the various halves of the cards and set them out before the children.
2. Pick up two non-matching halves of cards and try to join them together, ask the children why they do not join.
3. Point out the numeral on one side of the card, the number of smaller felt shapes on the back, as well as the shape of the card itself. Explain that there are several ways to determine if the card halves match one another.
4. Challenge the children to sort through and match the halves of the various cards.

TEACHER-TO-TEACHER TIP

- Challenge the children further by making the dividing line identical for each card. Children may not be able to match both puzzle halves correctly by sight alone. This increases both the difficulty and cognition levels a bit higher.

ASSESSMENT

To assess the children's learning, consider the following:
- Can the child use the numeral on the front of the cards to match like halves?
- Can the child use the number of shapes on the back of the card to match like halves?
- Can the child use the shapes of the cards themselves to match like halves?

Children's Books

Color Zoo by
Lois Ehlert
The Shape of Things by
Dayle Ann Dodds

Kay Flowers, Summerfield, OH

Patchwork Shapes

LEARNING OBJECTIVES

The children will:
1. Sort and classify shapes.
2. Recognize geometric shapes and structures in the environment.
3. Demonstrate the ability to cooperate with others.

Materials

cards (sample picture word cards: clock, doorknob, box, pillow (round and square), tub or shower, window, ruler, suitcase, rubber band, clothespin, drum, steering wheel, bunny's tail, turtle, stair step)
bag
paper and marker

VOCABULARY

curves	diamond	rectangle	star
corners	game	sort	triangle
circle	oval	square	

PREPARATION

- Cut out and laminate the cards and game board. Store them in a bag.
- Create a two-column chart. Label one column "corners" and draw an object that has corners, such as a book, at the top of this column. Label the other column "curvy" and draw an object that is curvy, such as a button, at the top of this column.

WHAT TO DO

1. Set out the cards before the children. Introduce them to a few of the objects on the cards. Ask the children to describe the shapes of the objects on the cards you show them. Ask, "Is it curvy or does it have corners?"
2. After the children decide whether the object has corners or is curvy, set the card in one of two columns.
3. Go through a few cards like this with the children, and then encourage the children to take turns picking up the cards themselves, identifying the objects on the cards, and then deciding whether the cards should be in the corners column or the curves column.
4. Let them continue to play until they are out of cards. Then, help the children shuffle the cards and repeat the activity.

ASSESSMENT

To assess the children's learning, consider the following:
- Can the child identify the objects on the cards?
- Can the child correctly determine whether the objects are curvy or have corners?
- Can the child put the cards in the correct rows?

Carol Hupp, Farmersville, IL

Children's Books

I Spy Shapes in Art by Lucy Micklethwait
The Shape of Things by Dayle Ann Dodds

Round or Square?

4+

LEARNING OBJECTIVES

The children will:

1. Look at pictures of objects and talk about the objects' shapes.
2. Classify pictures of objects by their shape characteristics.
3. Distinguish between round and square objects.
4. Create a chart of their findings.

Materials

large poster board
pictures of objects
   from computer
   clip art or
   magazines

VOCABULARY

chart	round	sort
classify	shape	square

PREPARATION

- Cut or print pictures that are round or square. Make sure there are enough for each child to have one.
- Draw a line down the middle of the poster board to make a two-column chart.
- Title the columns with "Things that are round" and the other with "Things that are square." Draw a picture for "round" and "square."
- Place the pictures in a bag or a basket.

WHAT TO DO

1. Gather the children. Show them the chart and talk about the shapes on it.
2. Give each child a picture and let him describe the shape.
3. Ask all the children if they think that their objects are round or square.
4. Give each child a piece of tape to place his picture in the appropriate column on the chart.
5. When all of the children have had a turn, talk with the children about objects that are round and square.
6. When the chart is complete, display it in the math area.

TEACHER-TO-TEACHER TIPS

- When the children are ready, create a chart with three shapes: circle, square, and triangle.
- Consider doing this activity with real objects in the classroom instead of pictures.

Children's Books

What Is a Square? by Rebecca Dotlich
What Is Round? by Rebecca Dotlich

ASSESSMENT

To assess the children's learning, consider the following:

- Can the child identify the featured shapes in the environment?
- Can the child classify other objects in the classroom by shape?

Shelley Hoster, Norcross, GA

Shake It Up!

4+

LEARNING OBJECTIVES

The children will:

1. Learn to identify circles, squares, triangles, and rectangles.
2. Learn a new game.

Materials

egg carton
permanent marker
  with a fine tip
  (adult only)
die (or small
  counter or coin)
4" tagboard
  shapes, 8 each:
  circles, squares,
  triangles, and
  rectangles

VOCABULARY

circle	rectangle	square	triangle

PREPARATION

- Cut 4" tagboard shapes, making eight of each: circles, squares, triangles, and rectangles.
- Mark the bottom of the inside cups of the egg carton with two circles, two squares, two triangles, two rectangles, two stars, and leave two without any marks.

WHAT TO DO

1. Explain to the children that the object of this game is to get rid of all your shapes.
2. Shuffle the shapes and deal them out to the players.
3. Show the players the egg carton. Explain that when a player shakes the carton and opens it, he must keep it flat on the table to see where the die or counter landed.
4. Ask the first player to put the die or counter into the carton, close it, and shake it up. Remind him to put it on the table to open it and see where the die landed.
5. If it lands on a shape, the player puts one matching tagboard shape in the center of the table. If it lands on a star, he gets another turn. If it lands on an empty cup, he loses his turn.
6. For a faster game, ask all the players to put shapes into the game pile every time someone shakes the egg carton.

ASSESSMENT

To assess the children's learning, consider the following:

- Can the child name the shapes?
- Can the child follow the game's directions?

Susan Oldham Hill, Lakeland, FL

Children's Books

My Very First Book of Shapes by Eric Carle
Shapes, Shapes, Shapes by Tana Hoban
When a Line Bends...A Shape Begins by Rhonda Gowler Greene

Shape Hunt

LEARNING OBJECTIVES

The children will:

1. Describe and compare three-dimensional objects.
2. Construct graphs using real objects or pictures in order to answer questions.
3. Follow simple directions.

Materials

class poster for
   graph
tape
3" x 5" pieces of
   paper (two per
   child)
pencils
three-dimensional
   shapes
precut shapes

VOCABULARY

compare   hunt   shape names   solid names
graph

PREPARATION

● Construct an eight-column bar graph.
● Label each heading for one of the two-dimensional and three-dimensional shapes one for another. Leave squares for the 3" x 5" papers.
● Hang the empty graph in meeting area.
● Gather the precut shapes and replicas of the three-dimensional shapes.

WHAT TO DO

1. Announce to the children that they are going on a shape hunt in their room.
2. Review the shapes they are to look for.
3. Explain that after hunting, the children will draw some of the shapes they discovered.
4. Hand out precut shapes to the children who want to remember what to look for. Allow the children to look for shapes.
5. Come back to meeting place.
6. Collect the precut shapes from the children.
7. Pass out two 3" x 5" papers and pencils to the children. Have them draw the shapes they found during the hunt.
8. Make a graph of the children's findings, using their 3" x 5" papers to fill the graph.

ASSESSMENT

To assess the children's learning, consider the following:

● Can the children compare attributes of real life objects?
● Can the children help construct a graph?
● Can the children follow directions?

Children's Books

Brown Rabbit's Shape Book by Alan Baker
Fuzzy Yellow Ducklings : Fold-Out Fun with Textures, Colors, Shapes, Animals by Matthew Van Fleet
Secret Birthday Message by Eric Carle

Sunny Hyde, Austin, TX

Shape of the Day

4+

masking tape
colored
    construction
    paper
blocks

LEARNING OBJECTIVES

The children will:

1. Recognize basic shapes.
2. Learn the characteristics of different shapes.
3. Develop basic counting skills.
4. Recognize numbers.

VOCABULARY

angles	fill	shapes	triangles
circle	full	sides	
count	rectangle	squares	

PREPARATION

- Send a note home that the children will be learning about shapes and that you will be designating each day to be about one specific shape.
- Use colored masking tape to display the outline of the shape of the day on the floor. Present smaller sizes of the shape made from construction paper.

WHAT TO DO

1. Each morning for a week, show the children the different taped shape outline on the floor. Invite the children to fill the taped shape with blocks.
2. After the shape is completely full of blocks, help the children count out how many blocks it took to fill the shape.
3. Engage the children in a discussion about the characteristics of each shape. Ask them how many sides each shape has, and to compare the shapes to see which shapes required the greater number of blocks.
4. Each day after the children leave, change the shape outline on the floor to the shape for the following day.

ASSESSMENT

To assess the children's learning, consider the following:

- Can the child identify the block shape outlined on the floor?
- Can the child help count the number of block used to fill the shape?
- Does the child indicate that he has an understanding of the differences between the shapes from day to day?

Holly Dzierzanowski, Brenham, TX

Children's Books

All Shapes and Sizes by John J. Reiss
Listen to the Shape by Marcia Brown

Song

"Circle Game" by Hap Palmer

Ship Shape

4+

LEARNING OBJECTIVES

The children will:
1. Identify, sort, and name shapes.
2. Find objects that contain or are similar to basic shapes.

Materials

pictures of
   triangles,
   squares,
   rectangles, ovals,
   circles, rhombus
   (diamond)
large plastic boats
small objects in
   various shapes.
shape labels
marker
clear packaging
   tape or contact
   paper

VOCABULARY

| circle | rectangle | shape | triangle |
| oval | rhombus | square | |

PREPARATION

- On each boat, place a shape label. For example, put a triangle label on the boat with the word and picture of a shape. Use clear plastic tape or contact paper to place the label on the boat.
- Gather all the plastic boats, one per shape.
- Gather an assortment of small objects for children to sort onto shape boats.

WHAT TO DO

1. Display the shapes for the children.
2. Engage the children in a discussion about the shapes' names.
3. Use a couple of the small objects and model for the children how to sort them on the ships. Put each object on the ship that matches the shape of the object. For example, place a small rubber ball on the ship with the circle label.
4. After modeling this for the children, challenge them to put the objects on the ships.

ASSESSMENT

To assess the children's learning, consider the following:
- Can the children sort the objects onto the proper ships?
- Can the children identify the shapes by name?

Quazonia Quarles, Newark, DE

Children's Books

The Shape of Things by
   Dayle Dodds
The Shape of Things by
   Tana Hoban
What Is a Square? by
   Rebecca Kai Dotlich

Triangle Patterns

Materials

red, yellow, and
blue cut-out
paper triangles

LEARNING OBJECTIVES

The children will:

1. Recognize triangles.
2. Learn how to identify and continue a pattern.

VOCABULARY

blue   red   triangle   yellow
pattern

WHAT TO DO

1. Display the triangles and ask the children to name the shapes and colors.
2. Demonstrate an ABAB pattern with the red and yellow triangles, and challenge the children to continue the pattern.
3. Beside the ABAB pattern, begin an AABB pattern with the red and blue triangles, and challenge the children to continue this pattern at the same time.
4. After the children have continued the first two patterns for some time, begin an ABCABC pattern, using all three colors. Challenge the children to continue that pattern.
5. Create different patterns for the children to continue, and then have them design their own patterns.

TEACHER-TO-TEACHER TIPS

- Store the paper triangles in zipper-closure bags in the math center, and encourage the children to create patterns during center time.
- For an advanced challenge, suggest that the children count the number of triangles in each pattern, as well as the number of ABAB, AABB, and ABCABC clusters in each pattern.

SONG

Do You Know What Has Three Sides? by Laura Wynkoop

(Tune: "Mary Had a Little Lamb")
Do you know what has three sides,   *Do you know what has three sides?*
Has three sides, has three sides?   *A triangle, that's what!*

Children's Books

Party of Three: A Book About Triangles by Christianne C. Jones
Shapes: Triangles by Esther Sarfatti
Triangles by Marybeth Lorbiecki

ASSESSMENT

To assess the children's learning, consider the following:

- Given the paper triangles, can each child name the shape he sees?
- Display ABAB, AABB, and ABCABC patterns. Can the child identify and continue the patterns?

Laura Wynkoop, San Dimas, CA

Zany Xylophone

4+

LEARNING OBJECTIVES

The children will:

1. Identify the smallest item in a set.
2. Identify the largest item in a set.
3. Prepare a sequence, arranging the set from largest to smallest.

Materials

construction paper
in green, red,
orange, yellow,
purple, and blue
white paper
markers
glue sticks
xylophone

VOCABULARY

arrange   smallest   sort   xylophone
largest

PREPARATION

● Precut construction paper rectangles of the following sizes. Cut enough for
each child to have one of each color.
Red—2" x 1"
Orange—2½" x 1"
Yellow—3" x 1"
Green—3½" x 1"
Purple—4" x 1"
Blue—4½" x 1"

WHAT TO DO

1. Give each child one set of rectangles and show the class an actual xylophone.
Point out how the bars range from largest to smallest.
2. Explain that they will be making construction paper xylophones by arranging
the paper rectangles from largest to smallest.
3. Invite the children find the largest (blue) rectangle and place it on their left.
Then have them place the smallest (red) rectangle and place it on their right.
4. Encourage the children to sort the rest of the rectangles by size, largest (left) to
smallest (right).
5. Have the children glue this arrangement on a sheet of paper so that it
resembles a xylophone.

ASSESSMENT

To assess the children's learning, consider the following:
● Did the child find the smallest rectangle without help?
● Did the child find the largest rectangle without help?
● Did the child arrange the rectangles from largest to smallest?

Sue Bradford Edwards, Florissant, MO

Children's Books

Rectangles by
Dana Meachen Rau
Rectangles by
Pamela Hall
*Rectangles Around
Town* by Nathan Olson
*Two Short, Two Long: A
Book About Rectangles*
by Christianne C. Jones

Body Shapes

5+

LEARNING OBJECTIVES

The children will:

1. Describe, identify, and compare circles, triangles, rectangles, and squares.
2. Learn to follow directions.
3. Work and problem solve with a team.
4. Compare two objects based on their attributes.

Materials

posters with
images of shapes
on them

VOCABULARY

circle	group	square
compare	rectangle	triangle

PREPARATION

- Create an open area for children to bend, stretch, and lie down.
- Set up one poster for each shape in a particular part of the area.

WHAT TO DO

1. Read a favorite shape book with the children. After reading the book, discuss with the children the attributes of various shapes.
2. Separate the children into groups. Explain that each group will make shapes together with their bodies when they lie on the floor.
3. Tell each group which shape they are to create, and then send them to different areas of the room.
4. Allow the children time to discuss how the will create that shape with all their bodies. For example, how will the group of four friends create a square? Where will they lie down?
5. If the children need help figuring out how to make their shapes, refer them to the posters that have the shapes on them.
6. After the children have had time to practice making their shapes, give each group the opportunity to present and explain their shape to the rest of the children. Discuss the shapes as a class.

TEACHER-TO-TEACHER TIP

- When a group needs a challenge, have them create a shape that is not one of the basic four shapes. For example, challenge the group to make a hexagon or diamond.

ASSESSMENT

To assess the children's learning, consider the following:

- Can the children identify the number of sides for their shapes?
- How long does it take a group of children to create the shape together?

Sunny Hyde, Austin, TX

Children's Books

My Shapes / Mis formas
by Rebecca Emberley
Shapes by
Robert Crowther

Shapes in My World

LEARNING OBJECTIVES

The children will

1. Identify shapes in their environment.
2. Practice drawing shapes from memory.

Materials

clipboards (1 per child)
pencils
shape sheet to record their findings

VOCABULARY

environment   rectangle   shape   triangle

WHAT TO DO

1. Talk with the children about different shapes. Challenge them to name shapes and say how many sides they have.
2. Take the children on a shape walk around the school or in an area close to school.
3. Remind the children to look for shapes in the natural environment. For example, the children may see triangle signs and rectangle doors.
4. After the walk, return to the classroom. Talk with the children about the shapes they saw.
5. Hand out pencils and paper to each child. Encourage the children to draw the objects they saw on the walk on their shape sheet. Help the children label the shapes.

ASSESSMENT

To assess the children's learning, consider the following:

● Can the child identify by name the shapes he sees on the shape walk?
● After returning to the classroom, can the child draw images of some of the shapes he saw while on the shape walk?

Sherry Harper, East Greenwich, RI

Children's Books

I Spy Shapes in Art by Lucy Micklethwait
The Shape of Things by Julie Lacome
Shapes, Shapes, Shapes by Tana Hoban

Fun with Drums

3+

LEARNING OBJECTIVES

The children will:
1. Identify shapes.
2. Play with rhythm instruments.
3. Enjoy music.

Materials

plastic or
  cardboard
  containers with
  lids in various
  shapes
xylophone and
  mallets
assortment of
  metal pans, pots,
  or bowls
favorite class song
  CD
CD player

VOCABULARY

beat	music	shape
drum	rhythm	sticks

WHAT TO DO

1. Display the assorted container drums on the floor in one corner of the room.
2. Demonstrate to the children how to use their hands or the sticks to play each drum.
3. Encourage the children to explore each drum and then name each drum by shape.
4. Suggest that one child play with the xylophone.
5. Encourage the children to form a shape band as they play in unison.
6. Play the favorite class song and invite the children to sing and play along with the music.

TEACHER-TO-TEACHER TIP

● Place a different material inside each shape drum such as popcorn seeds, foam peanuts, cotton balls, or plastic 1" cubes. Invite children to listen and see if the sound is different when there is something inside each drum. Invite children to shake the drum for another musical sound.

ASSESSMENT

To assess the children's learning, consider the following:
● Can the child correctly name the shapes of the drums?
● Can the child use objects or her hands to make sounds?

Children's Books

D Is for Drum: A Native American Alphabet by Michael Shoulders
The Drum: A Folktale from India by Rob Cleveland
Drum, Chavi, Drum! / ¡Toca, Chavi, Toca! by Mayra L. Dole
What Is Round? by Rebecca Kai Dotlich

Mary J. Murray, Mazomanie, WI

Match and Sing

3+

LEARNING OBJECTIVES

The children will:

1. Develop a sense of music appreciation.
2. Differentiate between shapes.

Materials

pairs of paper
   shapes
carpet squares or
   sheets of paper
   11" x 18"

VOCABULARY

get	pair	together
match	shapes	two

PREPARATION

● Display the carpet squares randomly around the game area.

WHAT TO DO

1. Give each child a paper shape. Be sure each shape has a matching pair.
2. Teach the children this variation of the traditional song:

   The More We Get Together (Traditional)
   The more we get together, together, together,
   The more we get together the happier we'll be.
   'Cause your shapes are my shapes and my shapes are your shapes.
   The more we get together, the happier we'll be.

3. Invite the children to stand in the group area. As they sing, instruct children to walk around and find the children holding the shapes that match their own.
4. After the children pair up, have them sit down on a carpet square together as they continue singing.
5. When all the children are sitting and the song ends, invite select pairs of children to stand up and call out the name of the shape they are holding.
6. Once all the children are standing again, have them change the shapes they are holding with another child.
7. Begin the song again. Repeat several times.

Children's Books

Circles by Jan Kottke
Color Farm by
   Lois Ehlert
*Shapes: A Teaching
Train Book* by
Robert S. Storms

ASSESSMENT

To assess the children's learning, consider the following:

● Can the children match their shapes to shapes of their classmates?
● Can the children describe and talk about their shapes?

Mary J. Murray, Mazomanie, WI

Shake a Shape

3+

LEARNING OBJECTIVES

The children will:
1. Develop their music appreciation skills.
2. Improve their musical abilities.
3. Enhance their shape recognition skills.

Materials

empty boxes with
   lids
markers
empty plastic
   Easter egg
12" balloon
beads
transparent tape
masking tape

VOCABULARY

beat	music	rhythm	square
circle	rectangle	shake	triangle

PREPARATION

● Draw one shape on each box.
● Place the beads inside the deflated balloon and blow it up to about 4" in size. Tie and knot the balloon.
● Place one to three tablespoons of beads inside each box and the plastic egg. Tape the boxes and the egg at the seams.

WHAT TO DO

1. Show the children the shape shakers. Demonstrate how to move each shaker to make a sound.
2. Invite the children to sit in a circle formation. Pass the shakers around the circle and have children shake and identify each shape.
3. Select a favorite class song and invite five children to come forward.
4. Have the children shake the shapes as the rest of the children sing the song.
5. Sing the song several times until all the children have a turn shaking the shapes.
6. Challenge the children to pay attention to the rhythm of the music, and to shake their shapes in time to the song.
7. Engage the children in a discussion about the shapes on the boxes.

TEACHER-TO-TEACHER TIPS

● Create several shakers of each shape so a larger number of children can play them at a time.
● For extra fun, cover the boxes with colored shape-themed wrapping paper or decorate all the shakers using paper shapes, stickers, or other art supplies.

ASSESSMENT

To assess the children's learning, consider the following:
● Can the child identify the shape she is shaking?
● Can the child shake her shape shaker in time to the music?

Mary J. Murray, Mazomanie, WI

Children's Books

Is It Red? Is It Yellow? Is It Blue? An Adventure in Color by Tana Hoban
Shapes by George Siede
What's That Sound? by Lisa Ann Marsoli

Playing Instruments and Marching in Shapes

4+

Materials

- musical instruments (triangles, rhythm sticks, drums, tambourines, sand blocks)
- masking tape
- CD of lively music
- CD player

LEARNING OBJECTIVES

The children will:
1. Learn the names of instruments.
2. Recognize the shape of each instrument.

VOCABULARY

circle	instruments	square	triangle
drum	music	straight line	
flute	sand block	tambourine	

PREPARATION

- Set up a chart of basic shapes: circle, triangle, square, straight line, rectangle.
- Tape large circle, square, rectangle, and triangle outlines to the floor. Also use tape to make a long straight line.

WHAT TO DO

1. Gather the children together. Show the children the instruments. Say the instruments' names, and demonstrate how to play them.
2. With the children, review the names of the shapes on the shapes chart.
3. Give each child an instrument and encourage the children to practice playing their instruments. Talk with the children about the shapes of their instruments.
4. Put on some music, and invite the children to play along with the music.
5. Occasionally, stop the music, and direct the children to move to the shapes on the floor that match the shapes of their instruments.
6. Once at their floor shapes, ask the children to describe the shapes of their instruments.
7. Have the children come back together in a single group, trade instruments with one another, and repeat the activity.

ASSESSMENT

To assess the children's learning, consider the following:

- Can the child name the shapes of the instrument she is playing?
- Can the child go to the correct shape outline on the floor?

Carol L. Levy, Woodbury, NJ

Children's Books

Shape Land by Helen Wendy Cooper
When a Line Bends...A Shape Begins by Rhonda Gowler Greene

Shape Song

4+

LEARNING OBJECTIVES

The children will:
1. Gain an awareness of several basics shapes.
2. Visually recognize each shape.

Materials

one triangle,
  square, and
  circle
another set of the
  same shapes to
  be placed on the
  room's walls,
  one per wall
rhythm instruments
  (optional)

VOCABULARY

| circle | one | three | two |
| four | square | triangle | |

WHAT TO DO

1. Introduce the three basic shapes and say their names.
2. Invite the children to say the names and "air trace" each shape several times with you.
3. Line up the children and hand out rhythm instruments.
4. Sing the following song with the children. If available, let the children play their instruments throughout the song.

The Shape Song by Terry Callahan
(Tune: "Frere Jacques")

Is this a square? (point to the square)   *It's big and round inside and out.*
Is this a square? (point to the square)   *It's big and round inside and out.*
Yes, it is!   *It's a circle.*
Yes, it is! (nod vigorously)   *It's a circle.*
One, two, three, four same sides,
One, two, three, four same sides,   *Is this a triangle?* (point to the triangle)
It's a square.   *Is this a triangle?*
It's a square.   *Yes, it is!*
                                                     Yes, it is! (nod vigorously)
Is this a circle? (point to the circle)   *Its three sides make pointy tips.*
Is this a circle?   *Its three sides make pointy tips.*
Yes, it is!   *It's a triangle.*
Yes, it is! (nod vigorously)   *It's a triangle.*

ASSESSMENT

To assess the children's learning, consider the following:
● Can the child recite the song?
● Did the child play her instrument along with the song?
● When shown a shape, can the child identify it by name?

Terry Callahan, Easton, MD

Children's Books

A Circle Here, a Square There: My Shapes Book by David Diehl
I Spy Shapes in Art by Lucy Mickelthwait

Square in the Air and Circle Spinning 'Round

5+

LEARNING OBJECTIVES

The children will:

1. Discriminate between a square and a circle.
2. Develop their large motor skills.

Materials

4" x 6" index cards
(one for each
child)
markers
CD or tape
recording of
music
CD or tape
recorder

VOCABULARY

circle   shape   spin   square

PREPARATION

- Draw circles on half of the index cards.
- Draw squares on the remaining cards.

WHAT TO DO

1. Give each child one shape card. Explain that they will be playing a new kind of "Musical Chairs." When the music starts, they are to pass cards to their neighbors and continue passing until the music stops.
2. After the music stops, tell the children to hold the cards in their hands.
3. Say, "If you're holding the card with a square, hold your square in the air!" Demonstrate what to do. Next, hold up the circle card and say, "If you're holding the card with a circle, spin your circle 'round and 'round!" Demonstrate making a circle in the air.
4. Repeat the music and corresponding body movements several times until children can correctly identify the cards.

SONG

Sing "Ring Around the Rosy" with the children. Talk to the children about what kind of shape a ring is.

ASSESSMENT

To assess the children's learning, consider the following:

- Give the children a mixed pile of paper squares and circles. Can they divide the cards by shape into two piles and name the shapes?
- Can the children identify other objects in the classroom whose shapes are square or circular?

Children's Books

Shapes and Things by
Tana Hoban
Shapes, Shapes, Shapes
by Tana Hoban
*So Many Circles, So
Many Squares* by
Tana Hoban

Karyn F. Everham, Fort Myers, FL

Hula Hoop Jump

3+

LEARNING OBJECTIVES

The children will:

1. Identify circles.
2. Develop their large motor skills by jumping along a hula-hoop path.

Materials

8–10 hula hoops

VOCABULARY

| circle | jump | round |
| hula hoop | path | |

WHAT TO DO

1. Hold up a hula hoop and have the children identify and describe its shape.
2. Arrange the hula hoops on the ground so that they make a path. The path can be straight, curved, S-shaped, or circular.
3. Have each child line up at one end of the path and jump into the first hula hoop. Then have them jump into each hula hoop until they complete the path.
4. Once all the children have had a chance to jump through the hula-hoop path, rearrange the hula hoops to create a new path.

Pattern idea

TEACHER-TO-TEACHER TIP

● At the end of the outdoor play period, create a hula-hoop path that leads the children back to the classroom.

ASSESSMENT

To assess the children's learning, consider the following:

● Can the children name the shape of the hula hoop?
● Can the children jump along the path from beginning to end?

Laura Wynkoop, San Dimas, CA

Children's Books

Baby Eye Like: Circle by Play Bac
Circles by Jan Kottke
Shapes: Circles by Esther Sarfatti

Painting Sidewalk Shapes 3+

LEARNING OBJECTIVES

The children will:
1. Develop their small motor skills.
2. Develop eye-hand coordination.
3. Improve their shape-recognition skills.

Materials

sidewalk chalk
sand pails or plastic
   containers
   containing water
1" or larger
   paintbrushes

VOCABULARY

paintbrush   paint   shapes   water

PREPARATION

● Use the sidewalk chalk to draw an assortment of 12" or larger shapes around the playground or sidewalk area.

WHAT TO DO

1. Take the children outdoors.
2. Provide each child with a paintbrush, a piece of chalk, and a container of water.
3. Invite the children to move around the playground area and find a shape to paint. Help them write their names inside the shapes using the chalk.
4. Encourage the children to paint the shapes with water until the shapes disappear.
5. Suggest that the children move around the playground and talk about the shapes as they paint.

TEACHER-TO-TEACHER TIP

● If you have a lot of sidewalk chalk, invite children to color in the shapes with chalk and then paint over the chalk with water for some colorful fun.

Children's Books

Circular Movement by Lola M Schaefer
So Many Circles, So Many Squares by Tana Hoban

ASSESSMENT

To assess the children's learning, consider the following:
● Can the children consistently paint the different kinds of shapes?
● Can the children name the shapes as they paint them with water?

Mary J. Murray, Mazomanie, WI

Sidewalk Shapes

4+

LEARNING OBJECTIVES

The children will:
1. Learn to name a circle, triangle, square, and rectangle.
2. Learn to recognize shapes.

Materials

chalk
large expanse of
    sidewalk
index cards
markers
small bag or
    envelope
buckets
paintbrushes

VOCABULARY

circle	rectangle	square	triangle

PREPARATION

● Make shape cards for a circle, triangle, square, and a rectangle. Place these cards in a small bag or envelope.

WHAT TO DO

1. Help the children draw four of each of these shapes on the sidewalk with chalk: circle, triangle, square, and rectangle. Ask them to draw the shapes as big as they can.
2. Divide the children into four teams. Move about 20' away from the sidewalk.
3. Ask a child to draw out one of the shape cards and call out the shape's name. The children on that team run to the matching shape on the sidewalk.
4. Repeat until the children have drawn all the cards.
5. At the end of the day, provide water and brushes to wash the shapes away.

TEACHER-TO-TEACHER TIP

● Extend this activity by using masking tape to make large shapes on the rug inside.

ASSESSMENT

To assess the children's learning, consider the following:
● Can the children make the connection between their index cards and team shapes to the shapes drawn on the sidewalk?
● Use the shape cards to ask individual children to name the shapes.

Susan Oldham Hill, Lakeland, FL

Children's Books

All Shapes and Sizes by John J. Reiss
The Art Lesson by Tomie dePaola
Listen to the Shape by Marcia Brown
When a Line Bends…A Shape Begins by Rhonda Gowler Greene

We're Going on a Square Hunt

Materials

paper square

LEARNING OBJECTIVES

The children will:
1. Learn the song "We're Going on a Square Hunt."
2. Identify squares in their environment.

VOCABULARY

four   hunt   sides   square

WHAT TO DO

1. Hold up a paper square and ask the children to identify the shape. Ask them how many sides the shape has.
2. Tell the children they will be going on a Square Hunt. Explain to the children that they will be going outside to look for squares.
3. Teach the children the following song:

We're Going On a Square Hunt by Laura Wynkoop
(Tune: "We're Going On a Bear Hunt")

Teacher: *We're going on a square hunt.*
Children: *We're going on a square hunt.*
Teacher: *We're going to look for squares.*
Children: *We're going to look for squares.*
Teacher: *Are you ready?*
Children: *Yes, we're ready!*
Teacher: *Let's take a walk.*

Children: *Let's take a walk.*
Teacher: *Do you see a square?*
Children: *Yes, we see a square!*
Teacher: *Where?*
Children: *There!*
Teacher: *We went on a square hunt.*
Children: *We went on a square hunt.*
Teacher: *And now we're done!*
Children: *And now we're done!*

4. Once the children know the song, ask them to line up at the door and lead them outside.
5. On the walk, encourage the children to point out the squares they see. Sing "We're Going on a Square Hunt" while you walk with the children.

Children's Books

Color Zoo by Lois Ehlert
The Shapes Game by Paul Rogers

ASSESSMENT

To assess the children's learning, consider the following:
- Can the child say how many sides a square has?
- Can the child recall the squares he spotted? Can he name the places where he saw various squares?

Laura Wynkoop, San Dimas, CA

Signal Flag

5+

LEARNING OBJECTIVES

The children will:
1. Learn to identify a square, rectangle, circle, and triangle.
2. Develop their large motor skills.

Materials

yarn
scissors (adult only)
tagboard cards
   with one shape
   drawn on each
hole punch
markers
two sets of four
   12″ x 18″ flags
   with one shape
   marked on each
   flag
set of cards with
   these shapes:
   square,
   rectangle, circle,
   and triangle

VOCABULARY

circle   signal   square   triangle
rectangle

PREPARATION

- Make four 12″ x 18″ flags with one shape marked on each flag.
- Punch two holes in the tops of the tagboard cards. Thread the yarn through and tie for necklaces. Make one shape on each card.

WHAT TO DO

1. Explain to the children that ships use signal flags to tell important information because they are usually too far away from each other to hear voices. Tell them they will be playing a signal game using shapes.
2. Give each child a shape necklace and ask him to name the shape on the cards.
3. Divide the children into two groups and position them on opposite sides of the playground.
4. Give each group one set of the 12″ x 18″ flags.
5. Ask one group to signal with one of the shape flags. Those children wearing that shape on their necklaces would then run to the group holding the signal flag.
6. Next, let the other group signal with a shape flag.
7. Continue until all children have run back and forth several times.

ASSESSMENT

To assess the children's learning, consider the following:
- Can the children recognize the shapes on the various flags?
- Can the children connect their shape necklaces to the flags?

Susan Oldham Hill, Lakeland, FL

Children's Books

Boat Book by Gail Gibbons
F Is for Flag by Wendy Cheyette Lewison
The Sign Book by William Dugan

Shape Float

3+

LEARNING OBJECTIVES

The children will:
1. Identify shapes.
2. Explore at the water table.
3. Develop their oral language skills.
4. Understand the concepts of *sink* and *float*.

Materials

variety of small
    shape objects
    that sink and
    float
4 colorful plastic
    picnic lunch
    plates
permanent marker
    (adult only)

VOCABULARY

dry	sink	wet
float	water	

PREPARATION

● Use permanent marker to draw a shape on each plate.
● Place the shape objects in and on the water. Some will sink. Some will float.

WHAT TO DO

1. Encourage the children to select an object from the water, identify its shape and say whether the object sinks or floats.
2. Then have the children set the object on the plate with the matching shape.
3. Have the children continue until they remove all the shape objects from the water and put them on the correct plates.
4. Afterwards, invite the children to dump the items back into the water for the next group of children.

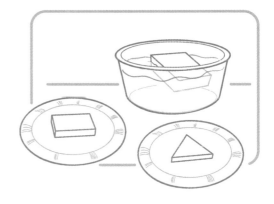

ASSESSMENT

To assess the children's learning, consider the following:
● Can the child identify the shapes by name?
● Can the child put the shapes on the correct plates?

Mary J. Murray, Mazomanie, WI

Children's Books

Eating Fractions by
Bruce McMillan
Give Me Half! by
Stuart J Murphy

Duck Pond

4+

plastic toy floating
   ducks
permanent black
   marker (adult
   only)
hand towels

LEARNING OBJECTIVES

The children will:

1. Identify a variety of shapes.
2. Improve their oral-language skills.

VOCABULARY

duck   shapes   swim   water
float

PREPARATION

● Use the permanent marker to draw
   one shape on the bottom of each
   duck. Let dry.
● Float the ducks in the water.

WHAT TO DO

1. Review four or six selected shapes
   with the children.
2. Invite small groups of children to
   work at the water table.
3. Encourage the children to pick up a duck,
   turn it over, and identify the shape on
   the bottom before placing the duck
   back in the water.
4. The children can examine several
   ducks in this manner and say
   the name of each shape aloud.
5. Encourage the children to work for
   several minutes as they take turns picking up ducks and naming shapes.

Bottom

TEACHER-TO-TEACHER TIP

● If you do not have a water table, simply fill a large baking pan or plastic bin
   with water.

ASSESSMENT

To assess the children's learning, consider the following:

● Listen and observe to see if the children are able to identify the shapes as they
   play with the ducks at the water table.
● Can the children count the number of ducks at the water table?

Mary J. Murray, Mazomanie, WI

Children's Books

*Little Chick's Friend
Duckling* by Mary
DeBall Kwitz
*Make Way for
Ducklings* by
Robert McCloskey

Guess the Shape

4+

LEARNING OBJECTIVES

The children will:

1. Learn about a circle, triangle, and square.
2. Identify a circle, triangle, and square by touch.

Materials

shape (circle,
    triangle, square)
    cutouts or
    attribute blocks
bucket of sand or
    sand table
blindfold

VOCABULARY

circle   shape   square   triangle
guess

PREPARATION

● If three-dimensional shapes (such as attribute blocks) are unavailable, cut shapes out of foam or cardboard.

● Bury the shapes in buckets of sand or at the sand table.

WHAT TO DO

1. Gather a group of children in a circle or half circle around the sand and water table or bucket(s) of sand.
2. Show the children samples of a circle, triangle, and square.
3. Ask the children what the differences are among the shapes. Discuss the attributes and names of each shape.
4. One at a time, blindfold each child and ask her to pull a shape from the sand. Make sure the child feels the perimeter of the shape.
5. Challenge the child to identify the shape. Give her clues to guide her to the right answer if necessary.
6. Repeat with the remaining children.

TEACHER-TO-TEACHER TIP

● Label each of three containers with one shape name and picture. The children can use these containers to hunt for shapes and sort them into the appropriate container as they find them.

ASSESSMENT

To assess the children's learning, consider the following:

● When shown two different shapes, can the children describe their differences?

● Can the children identify a shape by feeling it? (Consider blindfolding children to assess this.)

Jennifer Reilly, Grand Junction, CO

Children's Books

*Around the Park: A
Book About Circles* by
Christianne C. Jones
*Four Sides the Same: A
Book About Squares* by
Christianne C. Jones
My First Book of Shapes
    by Eric Carle
*Party of Three: A Book
About Triangles* by
Christianne C. Jones

Our Body Shapes

5+

LEARNING OBJECTIVES

The children will:

1. Identify the circular shapes found on the body.
2. Consider the different shapes on the body.

Materials

large sheets of
    paper, about 12"
    x 16" each
poster paint
pans
liquid soap
towels
marker

VOCABULARY

big   heels   small   toes
feet

WHAT TO DO

1. Clear an area of the floor in the classroom (or bring the children outside, if weather permits). Set out several pans of paint beside the large sheets of paper. Also set out a bucket of water with a squeeze bottle of liquid soap and towels the children can use to clean themselves with after the activity.
2. Invite the children to take off their shoes, step in the paint, and walk across the paper, making footprint paintings. **Note:** Make sure to have extra adults available to help ensure the paint stays on the paper.
3. After each child makes his footprint and the paint has time to dry, hang them paintings side-by-side at the children's eye level. Take care to line them up for easy comparison.
4. Ask the children to describe their prints. Talk about sizes of the prints; talk about what shapes the parts of feet resemble.
5. Point out the balls of the toes; explain that they are round like circles. Find the circular shapes on all of the printings. Ask the children to compare the circles on each print. Ask the children to trace with their fingers the circular shapes on the bottoms of their feet.
6. Outline the circular areas in marker.
7. Consider having the children walk heel-to-toe along the paper, making the outlines of shapes with their feet.

ASSESSMENT

To assess the children's learning, consider the following:

- Can the child identify the circle in his footprint?
- Can the child find other shapes in his footprint?

Karyn F. Everham, Fort Myers, FL

Children's Books

All Shapes and Sizes by
    John J. Reiss
Shapes, Shapes, Shapes
    by Tana Hoban

Press a Shape

3+

LEARNING OBJECTIVES

The children will:
1. Develop their small motor skills.
2. Identify a variety of shapes.
3. Develop their language skills.

Materials

modeling
  dough/clay
rolling pin
  (optional)
various shaped
  objects to press
  into the clay

VOCABULARY

clay	pin	roll
flatten	press	shapes

WHAT TO DO

1. Set out several ½"-thick lumps of clay for the children to flatten, either by hand or with rolling pins.

2. Invite the children to press an assortment of objects into the flattened clay, making an imprint of each shape.

3. As the children press a variety of shape objects into the clay, say the names of different shapes and ask the children to point to them.

4. When the children finish, have them ball up the clay into a fresh lump for the another child to use.

Lump of clay

ASSESSMENT

To assess the children's learning, consider the following:
- Can the child select the correct shapes when you say the names of the shapes?
- Can the child make imprints of specific shapes in the clay when you name a shape?

Mary J. Murray, Mazomanie, WI

Children's Books

Circles by
Mindel Sitomer
Pa Grape's Shapes by
Phil Vischer
Rectangles by
Sarah L. Schuette

Cut and Carry Shapes

LEARNING OBJECTIVES

The children will:
1. Improve their small motor skills.
2. Identify shapes.

Materials

sheets of paper
   with
   reproducible
   shapes on them
   (one shape per
   page)
child-safe scissors
paper lunch bags
paper punch
3' strands of yarn
shape stickers and
   art supplies

VOCABULARY

carry   cut   fold   shape names

PREPARATION

● Make several copies of the shapes pages on various colors of paper.
● Cut between the shapes, creating shape cards.
● Display the colored shape cards in a box or basket.

WHAT TO DO

1. Invite the children to select several shape cards and cut out the shapes.
2. After the children finish cutting out the shapes, help the children use paper lunch bags to create fun pouches in which to carry their shapes.
3. Show the children how to set a lunch bag flat on the ground and punch two holes through the bag, so each hole is close to the corners of the open end of the bag.
4. Model for the children how to string a piece of yarn through each pair of holes and then knot the string by each hole, to create shoulder straps.
5. Provide stickers and various art supplies with which the children can decorate the shape pouches. The children then put all their shape cutouts in their bags.
6. When the pouches are ready, lead the children on a walk through the classroom, challenging them to look for objects that match the shapes in their pouches.

ASSESSMENT

To assess the children's learning, consider the following:
● Can the child accurately cut out the shape outlines without help?
● Can the child string and knot the string to make a strap for the pouch?
● Can the child identify the shapes objects in the room using the shape pouch?

Mary J. Murray, Mazomanie, WI

Children's Books

*The Brambleberry's
Animal Book of Big and
Small Shapes* by
Marianna Mayer
Cut It! by
Henry Arthur Pluckrose

My Little Bag of Shapes

4+

LEARNING OBJECTIVES

The children will:

1. Control small muscles in their hands.
2. Classify objects based on physical characteristics.
3. Understand and follow directions.

Materials

small zipper-
    closure bags (1
    per child)
craft sticks (6 per
    child)
12" pieces of string
    (1 per child)
paper
pen

VOCABULARY

circle	octagon	pentagon	square
hexagon	oval	rectangle	triangle

PREPARATION

● Write the following on a sheet of paper. Draw the shape described in each line. Make a copy for each child.

Can You Do What I Do? by Freya Zellerhoff
Can you do what I do?
I can make a circle as round as a ball.
I can make a triangle, it has three sides.
I can make a square; all sides are just the same.
I can make a rectangle that has two long sides and two short sides.
I can make an oval, shaped like an egg.
And if you want me to, I make a hexagon with six sides for you!

WHAT TO DO

1. Talk with the children about different kinds of shapes. Explain the difference between a circle and an oval, and a square and a rectangle. Go over the text and images on the sheets of paper.
2. Hand out six craft sticks and one piece of string to each child. Encourage them to experiment constructing different shapes.
3. Challenge the children to make a circle, triangle, square, rectangle, oval, and hexagon. Help them if necessary.
4. At the end of this activity, hand out the bags for the children. They place their craft sticks, pieces of string, and poem in the bags so they can take "little bags of shapes" home.

Children's Books

A Circle Here, a Square There: My Shapes Book by David Diehl
The Shape of Things by Ann Dayle Dodds

ASSESSMENT

To assess the children's learning, consider the following:

● Can the child make the shapes identified on the piece of paper?
● Can the child identify the name the shapes she makes?

Freya Zellerhoff, Towson, MD

Peekaboo Shape Hunters 4+

LEARNING OBJECTIVES

The children will:
1. Learn to recognize shapes within complex shapes.
2. Improve concentration skills.
3. Improve small motor skills.

Materials

white cardstock
   6" x 6" (1 per child)
marker
scissors (adult only)
child-safe scissors
templates

VOCABULARY

circle	hunter	peekaboo	square
diamond	match	shape	triangle

PREPARATION

● In the center of each piece of cardstock, draw a square, circle, triangle, or diamond, each about 3" in size.
● Cut these shapes out for the children.
● Draw the shape a second time around the center of the first shape you cut out. For example, cut out a circle and then draw another circle inside the cutout circle. This is the line the children will cut along to make their Peekaboo Shape Hunters.

WHAT TO DO

1. Tell the children that they will be making a Peekaboo Shape Hunter.
2. Help the children cut along the second shape drawing. Each child should then have a shape within a shape.
3. Show the children how to hold their Peekaboo Shape Hunter up to their eyes and look around the room for matching shapes.
4. Encourage all the children with a square Shape Hunter to get up and look for different squares around the room. Do the same for the rest of the children with different shapes.
5. When the children spot a shape that matches their shape, they can point to it and shout, "Peekaboo square!"
6. Give all the children a chance to look for shapes.

ASSESSMENT

To assess the children's learning, consider the following:
● Can the child cut out her shape accurately?
● Can the child locate shapes that match her Peekaboo Shape Hunter?

Anne Adeney, Plymouth, England, United Kingdom

Children's Books

I Spy Shapes in Art by Lucy Micklethwait
Shapes, Shapes, Shapes by Tana Hoban
The Shape of Things by Julie Lacome

Sew What?

4+

LEARNING OBJECTIVES

The children will:
1. Identify various shapes.
2. Learn about the differences among various shapes.

Materials

cardstock
yarn (or shoelaces)
hole punch

VOCABULARY

difference	outline	shapes
identify	sew	trace

PREPARATION

- Cut the cardstock into large squares.
- Draw a shape on each square and punch holes along the shape.
- Tie one end of a piece of yarn onto each shape through a hole.
- Wrap tape around the other end of the yarn so that it is easier to work with and will not unravel. You will need at least one shape per child.

WHAT TO DO

1. Show the children all the various shapes. Talk with the children about each shape, helping them to identify the shapes by name.
2. Demonstrate for the children how to sew the outlines of the shapes in the pieces of cardstock by sewing the yarn through the holes. Invite the children to pick up a card and some string and try sewing the shapes themselves.
3. As the children are sewing the shapes, talk with them about the characteristics of the shapes.
4. After the children complete sewing one shape's outline, encourage them to trade cards with other children, so they can learn about other shapes.
5. At the end of the activity, ask the children to describe the different characteristics of the shapes they sewed.

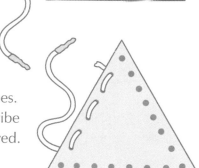

ASSESSMENT

To assess the children's learning, consider the following:
- Can the child identify by name the shapes that she is sewing?
- Can the child count the numbers of sides of the shape or describe other characteristics of the shape she is sewing?

Angela Hawkins, Denver, CO

Children's Books

A Circle Here, a Square There: My Shapes Book by David Diehl
Circles by Jan Kottke

The Shapes of Trains

LEARNING OBJECTIVES

The children will:
1. Identify circles and rectangles.
2. Learn the difference between circles and rectangles.

Materials

small colorful
construction
paper rectangles
and circles
large sheets of
construction
paper (1 per
child)
pictures of a train
engine and a
caboose

VOCABULARY

caboose	difference	rectangle	train car
circle	engine	train	wheel

WHAT TO DO

1. Show the children the
pictures of an engine or
caboose. Engage them in a
discussion about trains,
engines, and cabooses.
2. Ask the children to describe
the train cars and their
shapes. Describe the
rectangular and circular
shapes of the wheels and
cars.

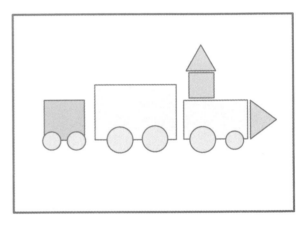

3. Let children choose paper rectangles and circles from a box to make
construction paper trains, including engines and cabooses. Provide help and
guidance as needed.

ASSESSMENT

To assess the children's learning, consider the following:
● Can the child identify the shapes on the train?
● Can the child create an engine or caboose with the construction paper
shapes?

Karyn F. Everham, Fort Myers, FL

Children's Books

*Engine Engine
Number Nine* by
Stephanie Calmenson
*The Little Engine That
Could* by Watty Piper
*So Many Circles, So
Many Squares* and
Shapes and Things by
Tana Hoban
Trains by
Anne Rockwell
Trains by Gail Gibbons
Train Song by
Diane Siebert

Trucks Are Rectangles, Squares, and Circles

4+

Materials

several rectangular, square, and circular blocks
construction paper
pencils, crayons, or markers
2 large boxes
poster paints
several toy trucks with truck beds
8 square pieces of cardboard 12" x 12"
glue or tape

LEARNING OBJECTIVES

The children will:
1. Learn about rectangles, squares, and circles.
2. Consider the different shapes found on a truck.
3. Find rectangles, squares, and circles on objects in the environment.

VOCABULARY

cab
circle

rectangle
square

trailer
truck

wheel

PREPARATION

● Set the boxes on their sides and cut window and door holes in them. Use the scrap pieces to create eight wheels.

WHAT TO DO

1. Show the children how to make a truck bed by tracing the shape of a rectangular block onto paper. Similarly, show them how to trace the shape of a square block. Below these shapes, trace wheels.
2. Invite the children to name each of these shapes while constructing the trucks.
3. Encourage the children to pretend that the appliance boxes are trucks. Ask children to identify the shapes.
4. Together, paint the boxes and wheels. Attach the wheels with glue or tape to the trucks. Pretend to be a trucker with these and with toy trucks.

SONG

Sing "The Wheels on the Truck" to the tune of "The Wheels on the Bus."

ASSESSMENT

To assess the children's learning, consider the following:
● Ask the children to describe their trucks, naming the different parts and related shapes.
● Ask the children to find something in the classroom that is a rectangular, square, or circular shape.

Karyn F. Everham, Fort Myers, FL

Children's Books

Duck in the Truck by Jez Alborough
The Great Big Car and Truck Book by Richard Scarry
Truck Song by Diane Siebert

Circles

LEARNING OBJECTIVES

The children will:
1. Learn about a variety of circles.
2. Develop their small motor skills.

Materials

old magazines to
   cut up
child-safe scissors
paste or glue
poster paper

VOCABULARY

big	crown	round
circle	ring	small

PREPARATION

● Place magazines, child-safe scissors, paste or glue, and paper on tables. You might cut out some circles ahead of time and place those on the table with the magazines, for the children to choose.

WHAT TO DO

1. Gather the children together at the tables. Tell them that they will be looking for things that are circles in the magazine. If necessary, show the children pictures of things that are circles.
2. Tell the children to flip through the magazines, find circles, and cut them out. Examples of circles include buttons, glasses, car wheels, steering wheels, coins, sun, pizza, pie, and cake.
3. After the children cut out their images of circles, help the children paste or glue their circles onto the paper.
4. Help the children write their names on the papers and display them on the wall.

FINGERPLAY

The Moon Is Round by Shirley Anne Ramaley
The moon is round. (have the children make big round circles with their arms)
It looks like me! (the children point to themselves)
A nose and a mouth, (the children wrinkle their noses and smile)
And eyes to see! (the children open their eyes wide)

ASSESSMENT

To assess the children's learning, consider the following:
● Can the child describe a circle?
● Can the child give examples of objects that are circular?
● Can the child manipulate the scissors and cut out circular objects from the magazines?

Shirley Anne Ramaley, Sun City, AZ

Children's Books

Around the Park: A Book About Circles by Christianne C. Jones
Circles by Sarah L. Schuette
So Many Circles, So Many Squares by Tana Hoban

Shape Factory

5+

LEARNING OBJECTIVES

The children will:
1. Learn to identify a square, rectangle, circle, and triangle.
2. Develop their small motor skills.

child-safe scissors
construction paper
markers
glue
small baskets or
   containers
tagboard patterns
   for a square,
   rectangle, circle,
   and triangle

VOCABULARY

circle	factory	square	triangle
create	rectangle	trace	

PREPARATION

- Cut and laminate some sample shapes so there will be plenty for the children to use.

WHAT TO DO

1. Explain to the children that they are going to work as a factory, which is a business that uses people and machines to make many copies of one item, such as a shoe factory or a doll factory. Tell the children they will be a shape factory, working to make many shapes to use for a picture in the classroom.
2. Explain that each child will trace and cut out one set of shapes: a square, a rectangle, a circle, and a triangle.
3. Ask the children to put all the squares into one container when they cut them out, and then put all the circles into another container, and so on, until they have all the shapes sorted.
4. Provide sample shapes so the children can trace the shapes onto paper and then cut along the line.
5. When there are enough shapes from the shape factory, give each child a whole piece of construction paper and a supply of shapes.
6. Encourage the children to create shape designs by gluing shapes to the paper.

Children's Books

All Shapes and Sizes by
   John J. Reiss
*Circles, Triangles, and
Squares* by Tana Hoban
*Pancakes, Crackers, and
Pizza: A Book of Shapes*
by Marjorie Eberts and
Margaret Gisler
Shapes, Shapes, Shapes
by Tana Hoban

ASSESSMENT

To assess the children's learning, consider the following:
- Can the child accurately cut out the various shapes?
- Can the child identify by name the shapes she cuts out?
- Can the child create objects with the shapes on the construction paper?

Susan Oldham Hill, Lakeland, FL

Fruit Shapes

3+

LEARNING OBJECTIVES

The children will:

1. Identify shapes, such as stars, hearts, circles, half circles, triangles, and ovals.
2. Explore the different shapes found in fruits and vegetables.

Materials

fruits (star fruit, oranges, bananas, apples, and so on)
vegetables (mushrooms, green peppers, eggplant, and so on)
knife (adult only)
cutting board
paper plates
chalkboard
chalk

VOCABULARY

circle	natural	shapes	trapezoid
eggplant	oval	star fruit	triangle

PREPARATION

● Wash the fruits and vegetables.

What to Do

1. Draw different shapes on the chalkboard. Tell the children the name of each shape. Explain that nature is full of shapes and that you will show them some of the shapes found naturally in fruits and vegetables.
2. Before doing any cutting, show the children each whole fruit and vegetable. Talk about the shapes the children see.
3. After you help the children identify the various shapes of the foods, cut each food in different ways to show the additional shapes found inside each one. Do not hesitate to cut each fruit and vegetable into unusual ways in addition to the way they are often prepared. Here are some ideas to get you started:
   ● star fruit: stars, trapezoids
   ● oranges: circles, half circles, triangles
   ● bananas: circles, ovals
   ● mushrooms: circles, tubes

TEACHER-TO-TEACHER TIP

● Suggest that the children use the cut-up fruits and vegetables to create food pictures before eating.

ASSESSMENT

To assess the children's learning, consider the following:

● Can the child identify the names of the various fruits and vegetables?
● Can the child identify various shapes in the fruits and vegetables?

Angela Hawkins, Denver, CO

Children's Books

The Shape of Things by Dayle Ann Dodds
Spookley's Colorful Pumpkin Patch by Joe Troiano
When a Line Bends...A Shape Begins by Rhonda Gowler Greene

Snacking on Shapes

3+

LEARNING OBJECTIVES

The children will:

1. Learn to identify and distinguish between shapes.
2. Develop their listening skills.

Materials

snacks in a variety
of shapes
(crackers for
circle and
cheese cubes for
squares)
plates

VOCABULARY

circle   shapes   square   triangle
rectangle

PREPARATION

● Create a snack plate for each child that represents each shape that they are learning about.

WHAT TO DO

1. Pass out the snack plates to each of the children. Be sure to tell the children not to try any of the food on the snack plates until you say so.

2. Engage the children in a discussion about the shapes of the snacks on their plates. Ask the children to identify both the names of the shapes and the names of the foods.

3. Tell the children to find and eat the circle food that is on their plates. Observe what food the children pick up to eat.

4. Continue in this manner until the children finish enjoying all the healthy snack shapes.

ASSESSMENT

To assess the children's learning, consider the following:

● Can the child name the foods he is eating?
● Can the child identify the shapes of the foods before eating them?

Erin Huffstetler, Maryville, TN

Children's Books

Color Zoo by
Lois Ehlert
The Shape of Things by
Dayle Ann Dodds
*When a Line Bends . . .
A Shape Begins* by
Rhonda Gowler Greene

Making Pudding Pie

4+

LEARNING OBJECTIVES

The children will:
1. Learn that pies are made in the shape of a circle.
2. Learn to look for other circle-shaped things in the classroom.

Materials

ready-made
   graham cracker
   pie crust
2 3.4-ounce boxes
   of any flavor
   instant pudding
   and pie filling
   mix
2 cups of milk
measuring cup for
   the milk
wire whisk
mixing bowl
paper plates
spoons
knife (adult only)
refrigerator for
   chilling the pie

VOCABULARY

circle	pie	pudding	bowl
round	piecrust	milk	spoon

WHAT TO DO

1. Show the children the piecrust and ask them to identify its shape.
2. Pour two cups of cold milk into mixing bowl. Add two boxes of instant pudding mix.
3. Let the children take turns using wire whisk to beat the mixture until it is thickened and well blended. This would take about two minutes of continued whisking, or longer with the children taking turns.
4. Help the children pour the mixture into a piecrust.
5. Put the piecrust into refrigerator and leave it there to chill for three hours.
6. At snack time, bring out the pie. When cut, a 9" crust will serve 16 slim slices. Ask the children what shape the pieces of the pie resemble.

POEM

Shape Search by Jan Black
I'm looking for shapes.
Look what I found!
A pie is a circle!
A circle is round!

ASSESSMENT

To assess the children's learning, consider the following:
● Can the child identify that a pie is circular?
● Can the child identify that the pie slices are triangular?
● Can the child identify the shapes of other cooking-related items?

Jan Black, San Francisco, CA

Children's Books

All for Pie, Pie for All by David Martin and Valeri Gorbachev
More Pies! by Robert Munsch and Michael Martchenko
So Many Circles, So Many Squares by Tana Hoban

Marshmallow Shape Structures

5+

Materials

marshmallows
pretzel sticks

LEARNING OBJECTIVES

The children will:
1. Make representations of shapes.
2. Apply their knowledge of shapes to a new context.
3. Develop their eye-hand movement.

VOCABULARY

cube	rectangle	three-dimensional
pyramid	squares	triangle

WHAT TO DO

1. Talk with the children about shapes, especially triangles, squares, and rectangles.
2. Supply all of the children with marshmallows and pretzel sticks. Show them how to connect these materials to one another. Encourage the children to make marshmallow triangles, rectangles, and squares.
3. Ask the children if they can think of ways to expand what they made while keeping their basic shapes. Let them experiment.
4. Help the children visualize three-dimensional geometric relationships by showing how to make a pyramid based on a square, or a cube based on a square. Let them try to make the shapes themselves.
5. Encourage further logical and creative thinking by introducing more geometric structures and helping the children to build them.
6. Let the children eat their marshmallow and pretzel stick creations.

ASSESSMENT

To assess the children's learning, consider the following:
● Can the children create triangles and squares with the given materials?
● Can the children visualize three-dimensional relationships? Can they create a pyramid with the given materials?

Children's Books

Greedy Triangle by Marilyn Burns
The Shape of Things by Ann Dayle Dodds
Shapes, Shapes, Shapes by Tana Hoban

Freya Zellerhoff, Towson, MD

Fingers Make the Shapes We See

3+

Materials

construction paper cutouts of a circle, a square, and a triangle

LEARNING OBJECTIVES

The children will:
1. Identify shapes in the world around them.
2. Learn a new poem.

VOCABULARY

circle   square   triangle

WHAT TO DO

1. Gather the children in a circle. Show them how to make a circle by touching their index fingers and thumbs together.
2. Show the children how to make a triangle and square using their fingers in a similar way.
3. Tell the children you are going to teach them a poem, and that the poem goes with the finger shapes they just learned. Hold your hands up in a circle shape, and prompt the children to follow suit.

Circle, Circle by Sarah Stasik

Circle, circle, (hold fingers up as circle)
What do I see?
There is a circle
Very near me! (point to object that is a circle)

Square, square, (hold fingers up as square)
What do I see?
There is a square

Very near me! (point to object that is a square)

Triangle, triangle, (hold fingers up as triangle)
What do I see?
There is a triangle
Very near me! (point to object that is a triangle)

4. Now, put the circle, square, and triangle objects in the middle of the circle.
5. Ask the children to identify the shapes that correspond to each object.

ASSESSMENT

To assess the children's learning, consider the following:
● Have children repeat the poem, identifying new circles, squares, and triangles around them. See how many different shapes and objects the children can identify as they become better at shape recognition.

Children's Books

The Circle Sarah Drew by Peter and Susan Barrett
Round Is a Pancake by Joan Sullivan
So Many Circles, So Many Squares by Tana Hoban

Sarah Stasik, Roanoke, VA

The Shapes Song

3+

LEARNING OBJECTIVES

The children will:
1. Recognize and name basic shapes.
2. Learn a new song to an old, familiar tune.
3. Help make up new verses to a song.

Materials

no materials
necessary

VOCABULARY

circles	cubes	rectangles	triangles
cones	cylinders	squares	

WHAT TO DO

1. Talk with the children about the shapes of a variety of objects in the room.
2. Name a shape and challenge the children to identify various objects that match that shape.
3. Teach the children the following song:

The Shape Song by Jackie Wright
(Tune: "Mary Had a Little Lamb")

I like squares	*I like squares,*
Yes, I do,	*Yes, I do,*
Yes, I do,	*A napkin is a square.*
Yes, I do.	

4. Challenge the children to think of examples of each shape to make up new verses.
5. Repeat the song, naming other shapes, and challenging the children to think up different examples for each shape.

ASSESSMENT

To assess the children's learning, consider the following:
- Can the children recognize different shapes around them?
- Can each child wait her turn and participate properly in the organized activity?
- Can the children talk and listen in a large group?
- Can the children effectively participate in the singing activity?

Children's Books

Changes, Changes by Pat Hutchins
Round & Round & Round by Tana Hoban
Snuffles' House by Daphne Faunce-Brown

Jackie Wright, Enid, OK

The Circle in the Square

LEARNING OBJECTIVES

The children will:
1. Learn to identify a circle, triangle, square, and oval.
2. Learn a new song.

Materials

20 pieces of 9"
square pieces of
tagboard
scissors (adult only)

VOCABULARY

circle   oval   square   triangle

PREPARATION

● Cut the 20 pieces of tagboard into five sets of shapes, with each set having
one circle, triangle, square, and oval.

WHAT TO DO

1. Give each child one of the 9" shapes.
2. Teach the children the following song:

Shapes Are All Around Us by Susan Oldham Hill
(Tune: "The Farmer in the Dell")

The triangle takes a square,   *Shapes are all around us now,*
The triangle takes a square.   *The square takes a circle.*
Shapes are all around us now,
The triangle takes a square.   *The circle takes an oval,*
                                        The circle takes an oval.
The square takes a circle,   *Shapes are all around us now,*
The square takes a circle.   *The circle takes an oval.*

3. Choose one child holding a triangle to start. As the others sing, the "triangle"
child chooses a friend holding a square shape.
4. Next, on the second verse, the child holding the square chooses a friend with a
circle shape. Continue with verse three.
5. Start over with verse one, until all the shapes have been chosen.

TEACHER-TO-TEACHER TIP

● This can easily be extended by adding verses for star, heart, and diamond
shapes.

ASSESSMENT

To assess the children's learning, consider the following:
● Show the children the tagboard shapes and ask them to name the shapes.
● Can the children sing the song?

Children's Books

All Shapes and Sizes by
John J. Reiss
Listen to the Shape by
Marcia Brown
Shapes, Shapes, Shapes
by Tana Hoban

Susan Oldham Hill, Lakeland, FL

Five Little Shapes

4+

LEARNING OBJECTIVES

The children will:

1. Learn to identify a circle, triangle, square, diamond, and rectangle.
2. Learn a new fingerplay.

Materials

set of shape flashcards with square, triangle, circle, rectangle, and diamond on them

VOCABULARY

circle   rectangle   square   triangle
diamond

PREPARATION

- Make the chart for the fingerplay.
- Set out the flashcards. (Create the flashcards if necessary by drawing the various shapes on note cards.)

WHAT TO DO

1. Teach the children the following fingerplay, using the shape flashcards.

   Five Little Shapes by Susan Oldham Hill
   Five little shapes in the world today.
   Can you see them as you play?
   One little square is a window to the sky.
   One little triangle is the roof so high.
   One little circle is a cookie so sweet.
   One little rectangle is a cracker to eat.
   And one little diamond is a kite in the clouds.
   Can you say them all out loud?

2. Engage the children in a discussion about the meaning of each line.
3. Ask the children to find other items in the room that match the shapes the song mentions.

TEACHER-TO-TEACHER TIP

- Extend this activity by having round cookies and square crackers for a snack.

ASSESSMENT

To assess the children's learning, consider the following:

- Use the set of flashcards to ask each child to name the shapes.
- Can the children say the fingerplay?

Susan Oldham Hill, Lakeland, FL

Children's Books

All Shapes and Sizes by John J. Reiss
Circles, Triangles, and Squares by Tana Hoban
Curious George Flies a Kite by H. A. Rey
Housekeeper of the Wind by Christine Widman
Kite Flying by Grace Lin
The Kite by Mary Packard

Have You Seen My Square?

4+

Materials

set of four shapes
per child: circle,
triangle, square,
and rectangle

LEARNING OBJECTIVES

The children will:
1. Learn to identify a circle, triangle, square, and rectangle.
2. Learn a new song.

VOCABULARY

circle	one	square	triangle
four	rectangle	three	two

PREPARATION

● Cut sets of four shapes per child: circle, triangle, square, and rectangle.

WHAT TO DO

1. Teach the children the following song about the shapes:

Have You Seen My Little Square? by Susan Oldham Hill
(Tune: "Do You Know the Muffin Man?")

Oh, have you seen my little square?
It has four corners over there.
And four straight sides, my little square.
Have you seen this shape?
Oh, have you seen my triangle?
It has three straight sides and three
  angles.
Count these corners: one, two, three.
Oh, have you seen this shape?

Oh, have you seen my circle shape?
It's round just like a roll of tape.
No corners and no sides at all.
Have you seen this shape?
Oh, have you seen my rectangle?
Four straight sides and four angles.
Count the corners: one, two, three,
  four.
Have you seen this shape?

2. Ask the children to hold up the correct shape as they sing each verse.
3. Discuss each shape with the children, and challenge them to count the sides and corners of each shape.

ASSESSMENT

To assess the children's learning, consider the following:
● Show the children the tagboard shapes and ask them to name each one.
● Can the children say the number of corners each shape has?

Susan Oldham Hill, Lakeland, FL

Children's Books

All Shapes and Sizes by
John J. Reiss
Listen to the Shape by
Marcia Brown
Shapes, Shapes, Shapes
by Tana Hoban

March of Shapes

4+

LEARNING OBJECTIVES
The children will:
1. Learn to identify a circle, triangle, square, and rectangle.
2. Learn a new song.

VOCABULARY

circle   rectangle   square   triangle

PREPARATION
- From the tagboard, cut 9" shapes of circles, triangles, squares, and rectangles.
- Cut the crepe paper streamers in 18" lengths.

WHAT TO DO
1. Ask the children to choose a shape to decorate.
2. Give them markers to decorate both sides of their shapes.
3. Help the children staple some streamers to each shape.
4. Teach the children the following song:

> **Circle Races** by Susan Oldham Hill
> (Tune: "Camptown Races")
> *Let's go on a march of shapes: Circle,*   *Hold your circle high!*
>   *circle.*   *Wave it in the sky!*
> *Hold that circle in the air*   *Let's go on a march of shapes*
> *All around the room.*   *All around the room.*

5. Repeat the song, substituting other shapes for circles. Encourage the children to name the shape with each successive verse.

TEACHER-TO-TEACHER TIP
- To extend the activity, ask some children to march with rhythm instruments instead of shapes, using the musical triangle, a circular tambourine, a round drum, and so on.

ASSESSMENT
To assess the children's learning, consider the following:
- Show the children the tagboard shapes and ask them to name the shapes.
- Can the children sing the song?

Susan Oldham Hill, Lakeland, FL

Materials
tagboard
crepe paper
   streamers
scissors (adult only)
stapler (adult only)
markers

Children's Books

Circles, Triangles, and Squares by Tana Hoban
Listen to the Shape by Marcia Brown
Parade by Donald Crews

Shapes Are Everywhere! 5+

LEARNING OBJECTIVES

The children will:

1. Recognize basic geometric shapes.
2. Apply the shapes to everyday objects.

Materials

scissors (adult only)
tag board (1 piece per child)
large piece of posterboard
marker
pictures, transparencies, and other visual examples of shapes

VOCABULARY

circle	group	rectangle	square
cutout	hunt	shapes	triangle

PREPARATION

● Cut out the poster or tag board into circles, rectangles, squares, and triangles.

WHAT TO DO

1. Engage the children in a discussion about the shapes you cut out. Have the children look around the room for these shapes.
2. Divide the children into four groups, one group for each shape.
3. Give each child one of the large shape cutouts. These will show the children which groups they are in. (The narrator will need one of each shape as well.)
4. Recite the following with the children. Encourage them to come up with examples of the shapes:

Teacher: *There are many shapes.* (children in shape groups hold up their cards and jump forward as the teacher holds up their shape) *Rectangles! Triangles! Circles! Squares!*
Teacher: *We see these shapes all around us.* (show the children images of objects that are the various shapes and have them call out their shape names when they see them)
Teacher: *A rectangle can make a…*
Children: *Bed! Door!*
Teacher: *A triangle can make an…*

Children: *Ice cream cone! Pizza!*
Teacher: *A circle can make a…*
Children: *Penny! Ball!*
Teacher: *A square can make a…*
Children: *Window! Block!*
Teacher: *So many things are made with shapes!* (hold up shapes so the children can call out their names)
Children: *Rectangle! Triangle! Circle! Square!*
Look around! (children point in many directions)
Shapes are everywhere!

ASSESSMENT

To assess the children's learning, consider the following:

● Can the children identify objects around the room that match the shapes?
● Can the children hold up the correct cards when you call out shape names?

Children's Books

Around the Park by Christianne C. Jones
Four Sides the Same by Christianne C. Jones
Two Short, Two Long by Christianne C. Jones

Terry Callahan, Easton, MD

Index of Children's Books

Index

ISBN 978-0-87659-088-1
Gryphon House | 13467 | PB

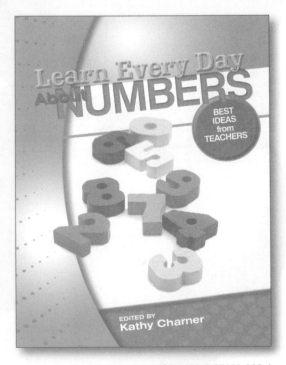

ISBN 978-0-87659-090-4
Gryphon House | 15573 | PB

ISBN 978-0-87659-237-3
Gryphon House | 13963 | PB

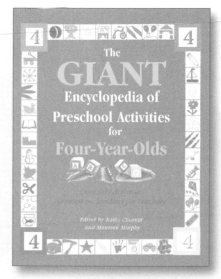

ISBN 978-0-87659-238-0
Gryphon House | 14964 | PB

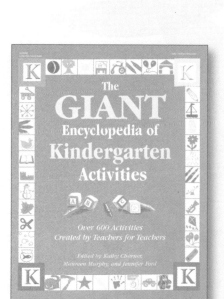

ISBN 978-0-87659-285-4
Gryphon House | 18595 | PB

ISBN 978-0-87659-013-3
Gryphon House | 13614 | PB

ISBN 978-0-87659-044-7
Gryphon House | 16948 | PB

ISBN 978-0-87659-166-6
Gryphon House | 19216 | PB

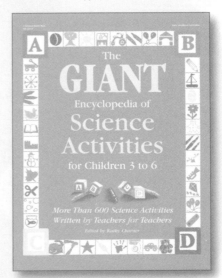

ISBN 978-0-87659-193-2
Gryphon House | 18325 | PB

ISBN 978-0-87659-181-9
Gryphon House | 16413 | PB

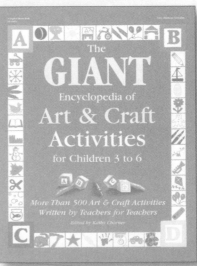

ISBN 978-0-87659-209-0
Gryphon House | 16854 | PB

ISBN 978-0-87659-068-3
Gryphon House | 18345 | PB

ISBN 978-0-87659-012-6
Gryphon House | 15002 | PB

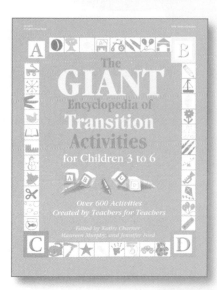

ISBN 978-0-87659-003-4
Gryphon House | 12635 | PB

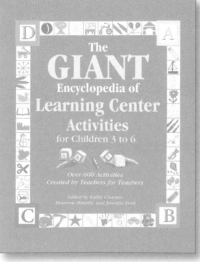

ISBN 978-0-87659-001-0
Gryphon House | 11325 | PB